Assembly Language Programming For the Apple II®

By Robert Mottola

Osborne/McGraw-Hill
Berkeley, California

Published by
Osborne/McGraw-Hill
630 Bancroft Way
Berkeley, California 94710
USA

For information on other Osborne books, translations
and distributors outside of the U.S.A., please write
Osborne/McGraw-Hill at the above address.

Apple, Apple II, Apple II Plus, and Applesoft are registered trademarks
of Apple Computer Inc. *Assembly Language Programming for the Apple
II®* is not sponsored or approved by or connected with Apple Computer
Inc. All references to Apple, Apple II, Apple II Plus, and Applesoft in
the text of this book are to the registered trademarks of Apple Computer Inc.

The LISA Assembler is a trademark of Lazer Micro Systems.

The S-C Assembler is a trademark of S-C Software.

**Assembly Language Programming for the
Apple II®**

ISBN 0-931988-51-9

 2 3 4 5 6 7 8 9 0 HCHC 89098765432

Cover design by Timothy Sullivan.

Contents

v

vi

Acknowledgments

There are many factors that could have easily prevented this book from ever seeing a printing press. Luckily for me, I know many talented people who've helped me get it all together. I'd especially like to thank Patty Henry for some serious amounts of typing; Nancy Wilson for proofreading; and the folks at Cyborg Corp. for putting up with everything involved. Also, special thanks to B. C. Bell, who booted me into this whole business in the first place.

RM

Introduction

If you've been using your Apple II computer for some time, you've had a chance to learn BASIC and develop your own programs. Although there were some frustrating moments, you managed to master the fundamentals of programming in BASIC, and succeeded in running your programs on the computer. Then you ran across the term "assembly language."

Maybe you saw an advertisement in a computer magazine proclaiming, "This program is superior to others because it is written entirely in assembly language." Or perhaps you noticed that a certain game program ran much faster than another because it was written in assembly language. You decided to learn how to program in assembly language. When you started to read about it, however, you were besieged with unfamiliar concepts — Boolean operators, symbol tables, pseudo-ops, mnemonics.

You shouldn't be intimidated by all these new terms. Learning to program in assembly language is no harder than learning to program in BASIC. In fact, for most people it is actually easier. Please note a primary law of computer programming: all computer languages are alike. They all have to do the same types of things so they all have the same types of logical constructs. Therefore, since you already know how to program in BASIC, you should find it easy to learn assembly language.

One of the problems with getting started in assembly language programming is that the majority of the books available on programming the 6502 are reference books. These, like the *Applesoft BASIC Programming Reference Manual,* are useful once you've learned the basics of the language. The purpose of this book is to instruct you in assembly language programming so that you can take advantage of these reference books. Also, the appendices of this book have more information which you will find useful once you have mastered assembly language programming for the 6502.

Appendix A discusses the 6502 instructions not covered in this book. The definitions are very terse, so if you'd like to use any of these instructions, you may want to read up on them in one of several general-purpose 6502 programming books mentioned in Appendix B.

All of the books listed in Appendix B cover the entire 6502 instruction set, not just the instructions discussed in this book. Also listed in this appendix are some other resources which can help in your assembly language programming.

Appendix C is a short discussion of assemblers for the Apple II, including important advantages and disadvantages. This information should help you make a choice on which assembler to buy, or which one to buy next.

Appendix D is a comparison chart showing equivalent assembler directives for a few different assemblers.

For those who want to put newly found assembly language programming knowledge to work immediately, Appendix E contains tips on how to interface assembly routines with the Apple II's monitor, Applesoft BASIC, and DOS.

Finally, Appendix F contains a chart of the 6502 instruction set.

This book is a tutorial and, like the Applesoft tutorial that probably introduced you to Applesoft BASIC programming, will guide you through some of the simpler assembly language programming procedures. Explanations are given with equivalent examples in BASIC whenever possible. The routines shown provide a relatively simple way to integrate the power of assembly language routines into your BASIC programs.

1
The Assembler and Hexadecimal Numbers

Before you can begin programming in assembly language, you'll need an assembler. An assembler is a program that converts 6502 mnemonics and operands into 6502 machine language code.

In simple terms, the assembler takes three-letter instruction "names" (mnemonics) and converts them into 8-bit binary numbers that the machine (that is, the 6502) can understand. Table 1-1 illustrates this translation process. For example, every time an assembler sees a JMP, it converts it to the hexadecimal number $4C. Whenever it sees a JSR, it converts it into the hex number $20, and so forth.

Although the assembler does a little more than that, what is important to understand now is that the assembler is a tool. With it, you don't have to remember all of the different numbers that the 6502 can understand. Instead, you just have to remember different names that comprise the 6502 instruction set (see Appendix F).

Several assemblers are readily available for the Apple II. A list and short description of some available assemblers can be found in Appendix B.

Table 1-1. Assembler translation process

Mnemonic (Name)	Meaning	Machine Language Value		
		Hex	Binary	Decimal
JMP	Jump to a new location (same as BASIC "GOTO")	$4C	0100 1100	76
JSR	Jump to subroutine (same as BASIC "GOSUB")	$20	0010 0000	32
RTS	Return from subroutine (same as BASIC "RETURN")	$60	0110 0000	96

THE HEXADECIMAL NUMBER SYSTEM

Like all other microcomputers, the Apple II uses binary arithmetic for all its internal operations. Unfortunately, humans don't. To compensate for this, programmers have developed a numbering system known as hexadecimal. Hexadecimal numbers are used because they are easy to learn, and they translate directly into numbers that the computer can understand.

To better understand this, consider the way the hexadecimal system works.

Learning hex isn't nearly as hard as you might believe. In fact, hexadecimal notation is easy. To start, understand that a hexadecimal number can be from one to several characters long, and, for the sake of clarity in this book, will always be preceded by a dollar sign. Be careful, however, for some programmers use different labeling conventions.

The following are all hex values:

- $00
- $1A
- $23B
- $FDAE
- $27E5

Note that all of these examples are preceded by a dollar sign to signify that they're hex. Also note that some of the characters are letters as well as numbers. Hexadecimal values not only use the digits 0 through 9, but also the letters A through F; where the decimal system has ten digits, the hexadecimal system has 16.

Counting in the decimal system, if you start at 0, you can count on your fingers all the way up to 9. After reaching 9, go back to the beginning and note that we've already been through the count once. This repetition puts the count into the ten's column. Each time we go through a count of ten, we increment (add 1 to) the ten's column.

```
ten's
| one's
↓↓
10, 21, 32, 43, etc.
```

Of course, when we run out of second-column digits, we just start another column.

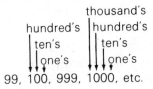

```
              thousand's
   hundred's | hundred's
   | ten's   | | ten's
   | | one's | | | one's
   ↓↓↓       ↓↓↓↓
99, 100, 999, 1000, etc.
```

As you can see, the digit in each new column is always ten times that of the previous column.

For counting in hex, let's say that we have 16 fingers instead of ten. Starting at 0, we could count 0, 1, 2, 3, 4, 5, 6, 7, 8, 9, A, B, C, D, E, F.

We used the letters A through F to continue the count after running out of numerals. Finally, at F we've run out of fingers. As in decimal counting, we start again at the beginning and note that we've gone through the count once.

However, to avoid confusing the hex value with the decimal value, precede hex values with a dollar sign, as in $10. Remember, this is the hexadecimal value $10; so instead of the 1 being in the ten's column, it's in the 16's column. We could keep counting this way, incrementing the count column each time we use up our 16 fingers.

```
  sixteen's
  | one's
  ↓↓
...$20, $30, $40....$A0, $B0, $C0, etc.
```

Just as in decimal counting, when we run out of digits in the leftmost column, we simply add another column.

256's
| ten's
| | one's
...$FF, $100, $101, etc.

Thus, the value of the character in each column is 16 times that of the column to the right of it. This is similar to decimal values where we have a one's place, a ten's place, a hundred's place, and so forth. In hex we have a one's place, a 16's place, a 256's place, and so forth.

Hex to Decimal

Converting a hexadecimal value to decimal is easy. All you have to remember is that each successive column's value is 16 times that of the next column. Let's convert $8D to decimal.

To convert the D in the one's column, we count to D on our 16 fingers to see that it has the decimal value of 13. Since it's in the one's column, we must multiply it by 1, which yields 13.

Next, we see we have an 8 in the 16's column. We don't have to count to 8 on our 16 fingers, since we are already familiar with what an 8 means. So, multiply 8 by 16, since it appears in the 16's column.

   $8 \times 16 = 128$

Now add the two columns together.

   $13 + 128 = 141$

Thus, $8D = 141. Now, try converting the other way around.

Decimal to Hex

Converting decimal values to hex is just as easy. Try the number 250.

Begin by assuming the hex number will occupy four places. We start with the last place, which in this case is the fourth, or 4096's place. Divide the decimal value by 4096 and get an integer answer. This would be calculated in BASIC as follows:

   PRINT INT (250 / 4096)

The answer is 0. Write that down as the value of the fourth digit (4096's place) as in the following: $0---. Since the answer was 0, try dividing the number by the next place, 256.

   PRINT INT (250 / 256)

Again, the answer is 0. Write down the following: $00--. Now, divide by the next place, which is 16.

   PRINT INT (250 / 16)

This time the answer is 15, so in the 16's column, write down the hex equivalent of the value 15, which is an F, as follows: $00F-. Finally, take the remainder of the above division, which is 10, and convert it to its equivalent hex digit, A. Put this in the one's column, and the answer will be $00FA. The leading 0s can be eliminated, so 250 = $FA.

Even though this answer is smaller than four hex places, it is a good idea to start the conversion calculation with the 4096's place. This is because the largest address the Apple II can access is $FFFF (decimal 65,535); starting with the 4096's place eliminates any chance of miscalculation.

2
Writing Code

To begin writing some assembly language code, we will need the following:

- 48K Apple II or Apple II Plus with disk and Applesoft in ROM, or Language Card
- An assembler
- A pad and some pencils
- An 80-column printer (preferred).

One more item would be extremely useful: the TI Programmer. This calculator performs the tiresome job of converting decimal to hexadecimal, and vice versa, and performs some logical operations as well as regular math. At about $50, it costs about the same as a good assembler (maybe less) and is the single most useful tool for computer programming, next to your computer. You should be able to get one at your computer or calculator store.

The pad and pencils are important to write down our programs first to assure they'll work when we try to run them. This also helps show how each line must be entered into the computer.

STRUCTURE OF A LINE

Consider the following section of BASIC code:

```
10 REM SUBROUTINE TO OUTPUT AN ASCII CHARACTER
20 B$ = CHR$ (CH)
30 PRINT B$;
40 RETURN
```

Obviously, no matter what is on a line, each line of BASIC code has two distinct parts — the line number and the instruction. Assembly language source code lines are also divided into parts, or fields. They have a place for both a line number and an instruction, but they also have a place (or a field) for three other things: a label, an operand, and a comment. Typical assembly language code might look like Table 2-1.

As can be seen from this example, each line of assembly language source code must have both a line number and an instruction mnemonic. Some lines also have labels, operands, and comments, but these are not always required. To find out why, each field will be discussed separately.

Table 2-1. Typical assembly language code

Line No.	Label	Mnemonic	Operand	Comment
1000	START	JSR	PRINT	;OUTPUT THE CHARACTER ONCE,
1010		JSR	PRINT	;THEN OUTPUT IT AGAIN,
1020		RTS		;THEN RETURN.
1030		END		

Line Number

Just as in BASIC, line numbers are used in assembly language as an aid to editing. For instance, in BASIC we can say LIST 100, and line 100 will be displayed on the screen. If we say delete (DEL) 200,400, then the lines numbered 200 through 400 will be deleted. The same is true in most assemblers.

Label

In BASIC line numbers serve another useful purpose in that they serve as targets in the BASIC code for GOSUBs and GOTOs. In BASIC we can GOTO or GOSUB a line number, but in assembly language we can do something even better. We can do the equivalent of GOSUBing or GOTOing a label. This feature makes it easier to see what the program is doing and allows the program to GOTO or GOSUB a routine without knowing exactly where it is by simply calling its name (LABEL). Most assemblers only allow labels to be six characters long, but they can be just about any combination of letters or numbers. That is usually enough to make a descriptive name for a location.

Consider the code shown previously in this chapter. The first two lines perform JSRs (jump to subroutine) labeled "PRINT." Even without the comments describing the function of the line, we could probably derive it just from the label. The reason is, of course, that the label tells what the subroutine does.

If, in BASIC, you saw a line that read GOSUB 2000, you'd have to look at line 2000 to determine what's going on. In well-written assembly language programs, the labels give a good indication of what a routine does.

To give an example of the power of labels, try some identification. Several useful assembly language subroutines are built right into the Apple II. Three that are stored in the F8 ROM have labels HOME, VLINE, and SCROLL. Without even looking at the code, it's easy to determine what function these subroutines perform. This is why labels are such a convenient way of identifying locations.

Remember, unlike a line number, a label is not required in every assembly language line. Only those lines that will be "branched to" or otherwise referenced will need labels.

Mnemonic

This field contains the instruction's mnemonic or operator. In 6502 assembly language, all instructions have three-letter mnemonics. These indicate the specific operation that is to take place. This is unlike BASIC, where the instructions are in the form of English words like NEW, IF, THEN, and so forth. Also unlike BASIC, assembly language allows only one operation per line. Every line must have an instruction, so this is not an optional field.

Operand

In BASIC, instructions like TEXT, GR, RETURN, and POP operate on their own. They do not change any data and, as such, do not require an operand. On the other hand, BASIC instructions like INPUT, GOSUB, or SPEED= are a little different in that they all need operands. A similar situation exists with assembly language instructions. This is not an optional field, then. An operand is required in the operand field if it is needed by the instruction in the mnemonic field.

Comment

Another good feature of assembly language is the comment field. This is a free field into which anything can be put. It is similar to the REM statement in BASIC, only it is available on every line. As with BASIC, good assembly language programs should be heavily commented.

> **NOTE:** On assemblers, the first character of the comment field must be some special character, like a (;) or an (*) depending on which assembler you use.

SUMMARY

Before proceeding to the next chapter a review of the similarities and differences between BASIC and assembly language is in order. Consider the following:

- Both BASIC and assembly language code have line numbers and statements.
- Each line of assembly language also has room for labels and comments.
- Assembly language statements are further broken down into mnemonic instructions and operands.
- In BASIC you can only branch to a line number; in assembly language you branch to a label.
- BASIC instruction words can be of different lengths, while all assembly language instructions are three-character mnemonics.
- Comments are important in both languages.

3
Entering
And Editing Code

Entering and editing code in BASIC is no more complex than booting up your machine, waiting for the BASIC prompt character ( ] or >), and starting to enter code. Editing commands like DELETE, LIST, and NEW are an aid when it's time to modify the code.

Text entry and editing in most assemblers is just as simple. The assembler described here, LISA, has text entry very similar to that of Applesoft BASIC, which is why it is used for most of the examples in this book. Be aware, however, that this is one area in which most assemblers part company. They all assemble mnemonics into machine code in a similar way, but their methods of text entry are generally quite different. The instructions in this chapter are given for the LISA assembler. If you are using a different assembler, you may use these instructions as a guide. When in doubt, refer to the instruction manual that accompanied your assembler.

The following is a sample subroutine that will give you some practice with your assembler. This routine will clear the Apple II text screen and beep the speaker twice. It is callable from BASIC or from the monitor.

```
1 HOMEBB  JSR      $FC58    ;JUMP TO SUBROUTINE AT $FC5B - THIS
                            ;WILL HOME THE CURSOR AND CLEAR THE
                            ;SCREEN

2         JSR      $FBDD    ;JUMP TO SUBROUTINE AT $FBDD - THIS
                            ;WILL BEEP THE SPEAKER
```

11

```
3        JSR       $FBDD      ;TWO TIMES
4        RTS                  ;THEN RETURN
```

The reason the program is so short is that it calls two machine language routines already residing in the Apple II monitor ROM — one that homes the cursor and clears the screen, another that beeps the speaker.

To enter the code, insert the LISA disk in the drive and boot it. After a display page is shown, LISA will be loaded and you will see the command prompt character "!".

There are a number of commands available from the LISA COMMAND mode. The ones used for this exercise are LIST, INSERT, DELETE, SAVE, ASM, CTRL-D, CTRL-E, and NEW. The following paragraphs describe each command:

- LIST — The LIST command in LISA behaves just as it would in BASIC. If you just type LIST, the entire program will be listed. If you type LIST followed by one space and line number range (for example LIST 20,100), just that line number range will be listed. Remember, there must be one space between the LIST and the first line number.

- INSERT — The INSERT command allows the entry of text into LISA. LISA automatically numbers lines starting with 1 and ending with the number of lines in the program. Thus, a 20-line program would be numbered 1-20. Since there are no "free" line numbers between any two lines (such as in a BASIC program that was numbered by tens), the only way you can put a new line between, say, lines 15 and 16 is to INSERT it. LISA not only inserts the new line, but also renumbers all of the lines from 16 to the end of the program accordingly.

  Use of the INSERT command is very simple. If you wish to INSERT code at the end of the program in memory (or, if there is no program in memory and you want to begin one), just type INSERT. LISA will then display the first available line number on the screen and allow you to type a line. It will print the line number for the next line and wait for you to enter it, and this will continue until you are done entering code. Then exit the INSERT mode and return to the COMMAND mode by typing a CTRL-E (for exit) followed by a RETURN.

  As mentioned, you may also INSERT new lines into an existing program. Using the earlier example, to INSERT some new lines between lines 15 and 16, type INSERT followed by a space and then by the number of the line which you want to insert the new code in front of. In this example, type INSERT 16, because we want to INSERT more lines before line number 16. We can say, then, that the command "INSERT 16" actually reads "INSERT (before line number) 16." As explained previously, when you are done entering lines, type a CTRL-E to exit the INSERT mode.

- DELETE — As in BASIC, type the command DELETE followed by one space and the range of lines that you wish to DELETE. If for example, we wanted to DELETE lines 35 through 45, we could type DELETE 35,45. Remember, the space between the DELETE and the first line number is necessary.

- SAVE — As in BASIC, to save your program on disk after it's complete, type SAVE (filename). When you want to retrieve your program again, use this command's complement, LOAD (filename).

- ASM — Once program editing is ended, you must assemble it into machine-readable code so that it may be executed by the 6502. This command allows that to happen. (This process will be discussed later.)

- CTRL-D — LISA allows you to execute any valid Apple DOS command from the COMMAND mode. Things like CATALOG, LOCK, VERIFY, DELETE, and RENAME are useful. To use any DOS command, first type a CTRL-D, then the disk command that you want. If you wanted to display the disk's CATALOG, you would type CTRL-D CATALOG and it would be displayed.

- CTRL-E — When you are in the INSERT mode and you want to exit and return to the COMMAND mode, you may type a CTRL-E as the first character of a new line. This will return you to the COMMAND mode.

- NEW — Again, like BASIC, if you want to scrap the program you have in memory and start over, use the NEW command.

NOTE: Most of the LISA commands do not need to be typed in completely in order to be used. For example, you really don't have to type out the word INSERT. Just the first letter "I" will do. For more on this, see the LISA user's guide.

One of the commands that can be entered here is INSERT. After typing it in, press the RETURN key and LISA will put a number 1 on the screen, followed by the flashing cursor. You are now ready to enter line 1. LISA's text editor uses automatic line numbering, starting with number 1. Every line entered will get the next available line number while in the INSERT mode.

The LISA text editor is a free-form editor, which means that you will not have to do much "tabbing over" to get all of the fields to line up with one another. With this editor, there just has to be one blank space between each field.

Enter the first line. The screen already has the line number "1" on it, followed by the cursor. If the first line of the subroutine is typed with one blank space between each field, it will look like the following example (note that LISA requires that the comment field begin with the semicolon character):

```
1 HOMEBB JSR $FC58 ;JUMP TO SUBROUTINE AT $FC5B — THIS WILL
                   ;HOME THE CURSOR AND CLEAR THE SCREEN
```

Before pressing the RETURN key, check the line to make sure everything is in order. Is there one space between each of the fields? Is the mnemonic (JSR) spelled correctly? Does the comment field begin with a semicolon?

If everything looks fine, press the RETURN key. One of the features of LISA is that it checks the syntax of each line as you enter it, just as Apple Integer BASIC does. If it finds something wrong with what is typed, a beep will result and an error message will be displayed. You will then be allowed to reenter the line.

If no error occurs, LISA will accept the line and print a 2 to indicate it is ready for you to enter line number 2. This line should read

```
2 JSR $FBDD ;JUMP TO SUBROUTINE AT $FBDD — THIS WILL BEEP
            ;THE SPEAKER
```

Remember, since there is no label on this line, a space must be typed before entering the mnemonic. If you don't, an error will result when you press the RETURN key. Again, once everything is correct, you'll see the next line number.

If things are proceeding smoothly, enter the remaining lines, but remember the spaces between fields. When you've finished entering text and no mistakes or error messages have resulted, your screen will look like this:

```
1 HOMEBB   JSR      $FC58    ;JUMP TO SUBROUTINE AT $FC58 - THIS
                             ;WILL HOME THE CURSOR AND CLEAR THE
                             ;SCREEN

2          JSR      $FBDD    ;JUMP TO SUBROUTINE AT $FBDD - THIS
                             ;WILL BEEP THE SPEAKER

3          JSR      $FBDD    ;TWO TIMES

4          RTS               ;THEN RETURN
```

Although all text has been entered, LISA is awaiting the next line. Since no more text is to be entered, exit the INSERT mode by typing a CTRL-E and pressing RETURN. LISA will now return to the COMMAND mode and display the "!" prompt.

Examine the code to be sure the assembler sees it the same way it was typed. Type the command LIST, and your text will be displayed. Notice it's been formatted neatly in columns. Except for the screen wraparound of some of the comments, it should look like the example subroutine. If it doesn't, or if problems have developed while entering the text, start over and try again. Just as in BASIC, the command NEW will clear the memory and allow you to start over. To verify that, type LIST. No code should be listed, and you're ready to try again.

Once the code is correct, you're almost ready to begin your first assembly. But first, the assembler must know where the code ends. Put the mnemonic "END" as the last instruction in the code. To do this, enter the INSERT mode by typing INSERT. This allows insertion of more code at the end of the present file. LISA will respond with line number 5. Enter 5 END. Remember to type a space before you type END to "pass over" the label field. Since END does not require an operand, and since no comments are needed on this line, press RETURN after the END.

Exit the INSERT mode with a CTRL-E. Back in the COMMAND mode, type LIST to make sure that everything is in order. The code should look like

```
1 HOMEBB   JSR        $FC58    ;JUMP TO SUBROUTINE AT $FC5B - THIS
                                ;WILL HOME THE CURSOR AND CLEAR THE
                                ;SCREEN

2            JSR        $FBDD    ;JUMP TO SUBROUTINE AT $FBDD - THIS
                                ;WILL BEEP THE SPEAKER

3            JSR        $FBDD    ;TWO TIMES

4            RTS                 ;THEN RETURN

5            END
```

If your code differs, it might be advisable to erase it all by using NEW and try again.

Once the code is correct, you should save it on disk. Label it HOME AND BEEP. However, add a file suffix, .SRC, to indicate that this is an assembler source file. The different types of files will be discussed later. For now, just call this file HOME AND BEEP.SRC. In order to save the program, type SAVE HOME AND BEEP.SRC.

The disk drive should turn on and the disk operation BSAVE HOME AND BEEP.SRC will be printed on the screen. Your first assembly language source file has now been saved.

If you wish, you may print out your listing on a printer. First, turn on the printer by typing CTRL-D followed by the familiar PR#1 command, assuming that a printer card is in slot number 1. Once the printer is turned on, type LIST and your listing will be printed. To turn off the printer, type CTRL-D PR#0.

4
Assembling a
Source Program

Two words that haven't really been discussed yet are "assembly" and "source." Since we are about to assemble a source program, a discussion of each is now in order.

BASIC, in reality, is an assembly language program located between $E000 and $F7FF in the Apple II computer. When you run a BASIC program, the assembly language program interprets the BASIC program by looking at each BASIC statement. For example, the following illustrates the program and its interpretation:

10 GR

"Time to turn on the LORES graphics mode and clear the screen."

20 COLOR = 1

"I'll set the LORES color byte for BLUE."

30 PLOT 10,10

"Want to plot a box? First I'll find the address of the tenth row, then I'll find the tenth column, then I'll put a blue box there."

Although the computer doesn't actually talk to itself, it does go through the same process of deciphering the meaning of a BASIC statement and then executing the appropriate assembly language code to perform the function. This is why BASIC is known as an "interpreter."

Assembly language works somewhat differently. The brief program written in the last chapter will never be executed directly, nor will it be interpreted by the assembler in real time.

To make it executable, it must be "assembled." Assembly is the process of taking those programs (called "source programs") that we can read and converting them into machine language object files that the 6502 can read and execute. When we finish an assembly, we will have our old source file still intact. In addition, we will also have the new, machine-readable object file. Schematically, it is something like the following:

Source Code ⟶ Assembler ⟶ Object Code

Again, nothing gets destroyed in the process, but a new file type is created.

Why couldn't an assembler just interpret source code, the way BASIC does BASIC programs? Why generate a whole new file type? From a practical point of view, the answer to both questions is speed. An interpreter could be developed that would interpret assembly language source code the same way BASIC interprets BASIC code; but, like BASIC, it would take a long time to execute. The machine language object code generated by an assembler, however, executes as fast as possible for the 6502. The reason for this is simply that this code is executed directly by the 6502, not by some intermediary interpreter.

Before actually assembling a sample program, familiarize yourself with these important concepts:

- Source code — This is the human-readable text containing the labels, mnemonics, and so forth, that an assembler will actually "assemble" into machine language "object code."

- Object code — This is the object of assembly. It is code in the machine language of the 6502 (that is, code that can be read directly by the 6502 microprocessor).

- Assembler — This is a program that reads in source code and "assembles" from it machine language object code.

ASSEMBLING THE SAMPLE PROGRAM

If everything has gone according to plan, the sample source code we discussed in Chapter 3 has been saved on disk under file name HOME AND BEEP.SRC. It is possible that the code is still in memory. To find out, type LIST. If it is still there, fine. If you've turned off your computer, you'll have to boot and load your assembler again, following the directions presented in the last chapter. Then type LOAD HOME AND BEEP.SRC to reload the source program into the machine. To verify it is there, type LIST.

You are now ready to assemble the program. Type ASM followed by a RETURN. The original program should be relisted, with a few extra items added to each line. If the entire assembly listing is not on the screen, generate another on the printer. To do this, turn on the printer, using the CTRL-D PR#1 for the LISA assembler. Type ASM again to generate the listing.

NOTE: In the LISA assembler, all disk commands other than LOAD and save must be preceded by a CTRL-D.

Use (CTRL-D) PR#0 to turn off the printer. If a printer is not available, check the listings provided.

Assuming that the assembly did not end in an error message, your first assembly language program has been successfully assembled. If the assembly did end in an error message, find out why. As in BASIC, assembler error messages are very specific and should pinpoint the problem. Using the instructions in the previous chapter, correct the problem, and try again. Your assembly language program should look like the following:

```
**END OF PASS 1
**END OF PASS 2

0800 2058FC   1 HOMEBB   JSR   $FC58   ;JUMP TO SUBROUTINE AT $FC5B
                                       ;- THIS WILL HOME THE CURSOR
                                       ;AND CLEAR THE SCREEN
0803 20DDFB   2          JSR   $FBDD   ;JUMP TO SUBROUTINE AT $FBDD
                                       ;- THIS WILL BEEP THE SPEAKER
0806 20DDFB   3          JSR   $FBDD   ;TWO TIMES
0809 60       4          RTS           ;THEN RETURN
              5          END


***** END OF ASSEMBLY

          *************************
          *                       *
          * SYMBOL TABLE -- V 1.5 *
          *                       *
          *************************

LABEL. LOC.  LABEL. LOC.  LABEL. LOC.

** ZERO PAGE VARIABLES:


** ABSOLUTE VARIABLES/LABELS
```

```
HOMEBB 0800

SYMBOL TABLE STARTING ADDRESS:6000
SYMBOL TABLE LENGTH:001A
```

Examine the assembly listings generated. They look similar to the original source listings, but they have two fields added. These are the "address" or "program counter" field, and the "machine code" or "hex dump" field, respectively. The "address" or "program counter" indicates the address in memory of the first byte of the machine language code generated by a line. The "machine code" or "hex dump" indicates the actual hex values that are in memory at that location. These two fields will be useful for many different things, some of which will be discussed in later chapters.

SAVING AND TESTING THE OBJECT CODE

Before attempting to run the newly assembled code, first save it on disk. Since it is machine language code, save it as a binary file. To do this, you must know both its starting address and its length. To determine both of these, refer to the listing. Look at the first line of the assembly listing. In the program counter field is the number 800. This is the starting address (in hex, of course) of the program. Look at the program counter field for the last line. It should contain an 809. This is the address of the end of the program. Therefore, to find the length of the program, subtract the starting address from the ending address, and add 1 to the result.

809 − 800 = 9
9 + 1 = $A

The answer, $A, is the length of the program. To save the object program, type (CTRL-D) BSAVE HOME AND BEEP.OBJ,A$800,L$A. Remember to type a CTRL-D before the BSAVE when using the LISA assembler. Note that the object code is saved using the same name as the source code, but with the suffix .OBJ. This practice is generally recommended because it keeps things easy to understand and allows you to determine which object file was generated from a source file.

Once the object code is safely saved on disk, it's time to run the program. If you are using the LISA assembler, type BRK followed by a RETURN. The Apple should beep, and the asterisk (∗) prompt character of the monitor will appear. Since the object code is located at address $800, type 800G. The screen should clear, the cursor should go to the home position, and the Apple should beep twice. If it did not work, something is probably amiss in the source program. Refer to the steps used to enter code in the previous chapter and reenter the code. Make sure all lines are there and make sure that the addresses in the operand field are correctly typed.

If everything worked correctly, you've learned how to use your assembler, write your first assembly language program, and assemble and run it.

GOING FURTHER

The following chapters will delve deeper into assembly language programming. However, now might be a good time to carefully read over the user's manuals that came with your assembler (particularly those chapters concerning the entry and editing of source code). In Chapter 3, only a few assembler commands were discussed. Most assemblers contain many other editing features that make text entry easy. You may not want to use them all at this time, but you should be aware of their existence.

Since subsequent chapters will discuss the various instructions and addressing modes of the 6502, it might be helpful to keep a copy of the assembler manual nearby.

5

Using Labels

In the program discussed in the previous chapters, you were introduced to the label feature of our assembler. Now let's learn how to fully use this feature. Consider the following program once again:

```
1 HOMEBB    JSR  $FC58  ;JUMP TO SUBROUTINE AT $FC58 - THIS WILL
                        ;HOME THE CURSOR AND CLEAR THE SCREEN

2           JSR  $FBDD  ;JUMP TO SUBROUTINE AT $FBDD - THIS WILL
                        ;BEEP THE SPEAKER

3           JSR  $FBDD  ;TWO TIMES

4           RTS         ;THEN RETURN
```

By using lines of the form

    JSR $FC58

it is not particularly easy to determine, especially at a later date, just what that line does. Instead, the following statement could be used:

    JSR HOME

This jump to the subroutine, entitled HOME, is much easier to follow than a simple jump to an address. Consider this BASIC example. A printer driver routine has been written and stored at location $300 (768 decimal). This printer driver is capable of printing not only text but LORES graphics as well. Consider the following ways to turn it on: CALL 768 for text, and CALL 782 for LORES graphics. In addition, to turn off the driver, there's a third call — CALL 802. The three calls must be used to deal with the hypothetical printer driver. To use this driver in a long BASIC program, many calls would be made to these various locations which turn on and turn off the driver. When examining the program, we'll either have to know just what these numbers mean or comment them well.

Consider this sample program segment:

```
2000   CALL 768
2010   PRINT "NEW PAGE"
2020   CALL 802
2030   CALL 782
2040   GR : COLOR = 1
2050   HLIN 0,20 AT 15
2060   CALL 802
```

It's reasonably difficult to determine what all these calls do, even though the references for these numbers are present.

Consider another method. Instead of calling the constants that represent each location, define those values to variables in the beginning of the program. For the sake of simplicity, give those variables logical names.

```
10   TEXTON = 768
20   LORESON = 782
30   OFF = 802
   .
   .
   .
2000   CALL TEXTON
2010   PRINT "NEW PAGE"
2020   CALL OFF
2030   CALL LORESON
2040   GR : COLOR = 1
2050   HLIN 0,20 AT 15
2060   CALL OFF
```

Obviously, this is much easier to understand. The names of the variables were chosen specifically to identify their functions.

This label format has another useful function. Suppose that the hypothetical printer driver had to be moved to another location, so that another machine language subroutine could be put at $300. This requires going through a long BASIC program, finding all of the CALL 768s, CALL 802s, and so forth, and changing all of them to the new addresses. Choosing the labeling format is much better. In this case, all that would be required is going to the beginning of the BASIC program, finding the three statements where values are assigned to the labels, and changing them to their new addresses.

The same is true with assembly language programs. It is much cleaner to define labels for addresses that are used in the beginning of a program. In BASIC this is accomplished with the LET statement. In assembly language this is accomplished with EQUATEs.

SAMPLE PROGRAM

Let's develop another short assembly language program. This one will print the word "ERR" on the screen, beep the speaker twice, and print three spaces, followed by no carriage return. Such a program could be used to signal an error. Like the previous example, this routine uses machine language subroutines that already exist in the Apple II monitor ROM. The routines to be used are

- $FF2D — Prints "ERR" and beeps speaker once.
- $FBDD — Beeps speaker once.
- $F948 — Prints three blanks.

Give these three addresses meaningful labels. Better still, since a complete source listing is available, look to see what labels Apple has already given to these addresses. The Apple II reference manual provides a complete source listing of the monitor. Following the program counter field, locate the addresses given above and find their respective labels. They are

- $FF2D — PRERR
- $FBDD — ?
- $F948 — PRBLNK

Unfortunately, $FBDD doesn't have a label, so one will have to be made. Looking at the code around address $FBDD, note a label BELL1 above it and a label BELL2 below it. Assign $FBDD the label BELL1A for use here.

It is generally advisable to use existing labels if using code that has been written and well documented by others. This labeling ensures that no one will be confused if they see your code because it refers to a subroutine that is used quite often.

The LISA assembler has two mnemonics for EQUATE. One is EQU which stands for "EQUATE." The other is EPZ, which means "EQUATE to Page 0." In the 6502, Page 0 in memory (locations $0-$FF) has special significance. Remember to use EPZ for any value less than $100, and EQU for any value from $100 on up.

Boot the LISA assembler, get into the command mode (!), type the INSERT command, and enter the code. If problems arise, check the instructions in the LISA user's guide, or refer to the explanations on text entry in the last chapter.

Here is the program:

```
1 PRBLNK    EQU   $F948
2 BELL1A    EQU   $FBDD
3 PRERR     EQU   $FF2D
4 ERROR     JSR   PRERR   ;PRINT "ERR"
5           JSR   BELL1A  ;BEEP SPEAKER
6           JSR   PRBLNK  ;PRINT 3 BLANKS
7           RTS           ;THEN RETURN
8           END
```

Remember, you need only one space between fields, but you must put in a space to skip over a field. If no mistakes are made, the code should look like the following as you enter it:

```
1  PRBLNK   EQU   $F948
2  BELL1A   EQU   $FBDD
3  PRERR    EQU   $FF2D
4  ERROR    JSR   PRERR    ;PRINT "ERR"
5           JSR   BELL1A   ;BEEP SPEAKER
6           JSR   PRBLNK   ;PRINT 3 BLANKS
7           RTS            ;THEN RETURN
8           END
9
```

Type CTRL-E to exit the INSERT mode, then type LIST to list the code. The listing should look similar to the original above, except, of course, for screen wraparound of the comments.

Long Comments and Blank Lines

To have a whole line of comments, not just comments in the comment field, put a semicolon (;) as the first character in the label field. The rest of the line can then be used for comments.

To put this new tool to good use, title the subroutine. To do this, insert more code at the beginning of the program. From the COMMAND mode, type INSERT 1. LISA will respond with the (new) line number 1. Type in the following header:

```
1  ;************************
2  ;THIS SUBROUTINE WILL
3  ;PRINT "ERR", BEEP
4  ;THE SPEAKER TWICE,
```

```
5  ;THEN PRINT 3 BLANKS
6  ;*************************
7  ;
8  ;
9
```

Lines 7 and 8 contain only semicolons and are used to provide blank lines for readability.

Exit the INSERT mode (CTRL-E) and list the code. Add one more thing to visually separate the EQUATE from the body of the program. Enter the following lines 11 and 12:

```
11  PRERR  EQU $FF2D
12  ERROR JSR  PRERR ;PRINT "ERR"
```

Separating the lines with some blank comment lines will make it easier to read. From the COMMAND mode, type INSERT 12 (which means, insert before line number 12). When LISA prompts you with the line number, type a semicolon and a return for each line, as in the following:

```
12 ;
13 ;
14
```

Exit the INSERT mode with a CTRL-E, then list the program. It should look like the following:

```
 1  ;************************
 2  ;THIS SUBROUTINE WILL
 3  ;PRINT "ERR", BEEP
 4  ;THE SPEAKER TWICE,
 5  ;THEN PRINT 3 BLANKS
 6  ;************************
 7  ;
 8  ;
 9  PRBLNK    EQU $F948
10  BELL1A    EQU $FBDD
11  PRERR     EQU $FF2D
12  ;
13  ;
14  ERROR     JSR PRERR  ;PRINT "ERR"
15            JSR BELL1A ;BEEP SPEAKER
16            JSR PRBLNK ;PRINT 3 BLANKS
17            RTS        ;THEN RETURN
18  END
```

If things are still working smoothly, save this file on the disk and assemble it. Use ERROR SUB.SRC for a file name. To save a source file, type SAVE ERROR SUB.SRC. The program will be saved on the disk. To assemble, type ASM.

Barring any errors in the source code, a complete assembly listing will appear on the screen.

Printing the Program

If you have a printer available, it is helpful to print the assembly listing for later examination. To turn on the printer, type CTRL-D PR#1, then type ASM to generate an assembly listing. Then turn off the printer with CTRL-D PR#0.

6
Making the Program Run At Different Locations

Here is a complete assembly listing for the sample routine assembled in the previous chapters. Carefully check it against the one generated on your assembler. Pay particular attention to the program counter field.

```
**END OF PASS 1
**END OF PASS 2

0800              1  ;************************
0800              2  ;THIS SUBROUTINE WILL
0800              3  ;PRINT "ERR", BEEP
0800              4  ;THE SPEAKER TWICE,
0800              5  ;THEN PRINT 3 BLANKS
0800              6  ;************************
0800              7  ;
0800              8  ;
0800              9  PRBLNK   EQU   $F948
0800             10  BELL1A   EQU   $FBDD
0800             11  PRERR    EQU   $FF2D
0800             12  ;
0800             13  ;
0800 202DFF      14  ERROR    JSR   PRERR    ;PRINT "ERR"
0803 20DDFB      15           JSR   BELL1A   ;BEEP SPEAKER
0806 2048F9      16           JSR   PRBLNK   ;PRINT 3 BLANKS
0809 60          17           RTS            ;THEN RETURN
                 18           END
```

```
***** END OF ASSEMBLY

        ************************
        *                      *
        * SYMBOL TABLE -- V 1.5 *
        *                      *
        ************************
```

```
LABEL. LOC.  LABEL. LOC.  LABEL. LOC.

** ZERO PAGE VARIABLES:

** ABSOLUTE VARIABLES/LABELS
PRBLNK F948  BELL1A FBDD  PRERR  FF2D  ERROR  0800
SYMBOL TABLE STARTING ADDRESS:6000
SYMBOL TABLE LENGTH:0032
```

As you scan the program counter field, notice that the value for the program counter on the first line of the program is $800, just as on the second and third lines. In fact, it remains at $800 until the first line of the body of the program, the line with the label ERROR.

As previously discussed, the machine code will be located at the memory address indicated in the program counter field. Remember that the machine language object code generated by an assembly will be read and executed directly by the 6502. Consequently, the reason the comment lines at the beginning of the program did not advance the program counter is that the assembler did not generate any object code for them. They are there only for the programmer's benefit, so the assembler skips over them, just as the BASIC interpreter skips over REM statements.

The assembler did not advance the program counter on the lines with the EQUATEs on them because EQUATEs, like comments, are not executable by the 6502. As can be seen from the object code field, no code is generated for these lines. But unlike comments that are only there for the programmer's use, EQUs are also used by the assembler. They are used to generate the symbol table that will be used in the actual assembly process.

To illustrate this, consider what the assembler does when it sees line 15 of this program. First, it sees the mnemonic JSR and assembles it into its machine language equivalent value, $20. Then, it sees the label BELL1A. It looks up the value of BELL1A in its symbol table to find that it has been given the value of $FBDD. It then places this value immediately following the $20 generated by the JSR. Looking at the object code field of that line in your assembly listing, you'll see the following values: 803   20 DD FB. Note that the two hex bytes of the address $FBDD are reversed. The 6502 requires two-byte addresses to be presented low-order byte first.

EQUATE does not really change the program counter because it generates no object code. In fact, the mnemonic for EQUATE isn't even in the 6502 instruction set. EQUATE, just like the END mnemonic at the end of your assembly, is called an "assembler directive" or "pseudo-op." It tells the assembler to do something, which is why it generates no object code. EQU tells the assembler to add a symbol to the symbol table. END tells the assembler where the end of the source code is.

Many different assembler directives are available for your assembler. A few of these will be discussed throughout this book. Look at your assembler user's guide to see what kinds of assembler directives are available.

CHANGING PROGRAM STORAGE

One of the most important assembler directives is the ORIGIN directive. It allows you to specify the starting address of your code. In the assembly listings generated so far, the starting address is always $800. This is because the LISA assembler defaults the program counter to $800 if the ORIGIN is not specified.

Specify an ORIGIN of $300 for the ERROR SUB routine. This will allow calling this routine from BASIC if so desired. The required mnemonic is ORG. However, it cannot be used alone. Once the assembler is told that the code is to be run at some address other than $800, it must be told where to generate and store the code during the assembly process. It is not practical to tell it to store the code at the same memory address at which it will run because the assembler itself is a reasonably large program, and storing object code in an area already occupied by the assembler should be avoided. Otherwise, an assembly-time crash might occur.

The LISA assembler has provided an area in memory to store code and it starts at $800. The mnemonic used to tell the assembler where to store the object code is OBJ.

Somewhere before the body of the program (just under the heading, for instance), insert the following new lines into the program:

```
ORG   $300   ;STARTING ADDRESS OF PROGRAM
OBJ   $800   ;LOCATION TO STORE CODE DURING ASSEMBLY
```

Remember, assembler directives are mnemonics and belong in the mnemonic field. Add lines of text to the source code and the new listing should look like the following:

```
 1  ;************************
 2  ;THIS SUBROUTINE WILL
 3  ;PRINT "ERR", BEEP
 4  ;THE SPEAKER TWICE,
 5  ;THEN PRINT 3 BLANKS
 6  ;************************
 7  ;
 8  ;
 9          ORG   $300
10          OBJ   $800
11  ;
12  ;
13 PRBLNK   EQU   $F948
14 BELL1A   EQU   $FBDD
15 PRERR    EQU   $FF2D
16  ;
17  ;
18 ERROR    JSR   PRERR    ;PRINT "ERR"
19          JSR   BELL1A   ;BEEP SPEAKER
20          JSR   PRBLNK   ;PRINT 3 BLANKS
21          RTS            ;THEN RETURN
22          END
```

Save the source code with the ORIGIN change on disk. Finally, assemble the new code and verify the assembly listing. As you can see, the value for the program counter changed from $800 to $300 on the line that contained the ORIGIN statement. The newly assembled code is ready to run at $300.

Before running it, save the object code on disk. Because the object code is in machine language, it must be saved as a binary file. To do that, calculate the length of the file. Subtract the value of the program counter at the first line of the main program (the one with the label ERROR on it) from its value at the last line of the program (the one with the RTS instruction on it), then add 1 to that. The answer should be $A. To save the object code, type

(CTRL-D) BSAVE ERROR SUB.OBJ,A$800,L$A

If you haven't made an assembly listing since you've set the ORIGIN at $300, now is the time to do it. The result should look like the following:

```
**END OF PASS 1
**END OF PASS 2

0800      1  ;************************
0800      2  ;THIS SUBROUTINE WILL
0800      3  ;PRINT "ERR", BEEP
0800      4  ;THE SPEAKER TWICE,
0800      5  ;THEN PRINT 3 BLANKS
0800      6  ;************************
0800      7  ;
```

```
0800              8  ;
0300              9            ORG   $300
0300             10            OBJ   $800
0300             11  ;
0300             12  ;
0300             13  PRBLNK    EQU   $F948
0300             14  BELL1A    EQU   $FBDD
0300             15  PRERR     EQU   $FF2D
0300             16  ;
0300             17  ;
0300  202DFF     18  ERROR     END   PRERR      ;PRINT "ERR"
0303  20DDFB     19            JSR   BELL1A     ;BEEP SPEAKER
0306  2048F9     20            JSR   PRBLNK     ;PRINT 3 BLANKS
0309  60         21            RTS              ;THEN RETURN
                 22            END
```

```
***** END OF ASSEMBLY

        *************************
        *                       *
        * SYMBOL TABLE -- V 1.5 *
        *                       *
        *************************

LABEL. LOC.  LABEL. LOC.  LABEL. LOC.

** ZERO PAGE VARIABLES:


** ABSOLUTE VARIABLES/LABELS

PRBLNK F948  BELL1A FBDD  PRERR  FF2D  ERROR  0300

SYMBOL TABLE STARTING ADDRESS:6000
SYMBOL TABLE LENGTH:0032
```

TESTING THE CODE

Pull the assembler disk out of the drive. Turn off the Apple's power. Turn it back on and boot from an Apple master disk.

Remember, even though the ORIGIN was set to $300 (the program is to begin executing at $300), the code will be generated and stored (BSAVEd) at $800. To use the program, just BLOAD it at its origin, $300.

Reinsert the disk on which the object file was saved and type

BLOAD ERROR SUB.OBJ,A$300

When the routine has been loaded, enter the monitor with CALL − 151. Before running it, type 300L. A disassembly of the code should start at $300. The first few lines should look similar to the program, except, of course, without any labels or comments, If they do, you're ready to run; if they don't, you'd better go back to make sure you actually saved the code and that it assembled correctly.

If everything is in order, type 300G. Now "ERR" will be printed on the screen, the Apple will beep twice, and three spaces will be printed.

These last few chapters have gone into great detail concerning text entry and editing. By now you should be familiar with the operation of the assembler. If not, review the previous chapters, because the remainder of this book will deal less and less with the operation of the assembler, and more and more with the assembly language of the 6502.

7
The Concept of Registers

Imagine a BASIC program in which the only arithmetic operations available were addition and subtraction. Further imagine that, along with the regular variables used in the program, three "special" variables were available — A, X, and Y. The reason that these variables are special is that they must be involved in all move and arithmetic operations. In other words, you could not use a statement of the form

```
10 M = N
```

but instead would have to use

```
10 A = N
20 M = A
```

You are not allowed, in this hypothetical BASIC language, to move the contents of one variable directly into another. Instead, you must move the contents out of the first variable and into the special "A" variable. The contents can then be moved out of the "A" variable and into the target variable. As another example, you could not say

```
40 Q = R
```

but instead could say

```
40 A = R
50 Q = A
```

The rules are the same for arithmetic operations. You could not say

```
100 R = S + T
```

but you could use

```
100 A = S
110 A = A + T
120 R = A
```

You could not use

```
200 U = V − W
```

but instead could use

```
200 A = V
210 A = A − W
220 U = A
```

This arbitrary, hypothetical BASIC illustrates the concept of "registers." The 6502 microprocessor has three data registers: the accumulator, the X register, and Y register. All memory-to-memory move operations must use one of these registers, just as in the hypothetical BASIC all move operations required one of the "operand" variables A, X, or Y.

A register is a special place in the microprocessor itself that can hold an 8-bit value. It's similar to an address in memory except that it is in the microprocessor chip. The instruction set of the 6502 not only contains instructions to load material into these registers from specified memory locations, but also has certain instructions that allow the contents of these registers to be modified in certain ways. With few exceptions, this is the only method by which the 6502 can perform any arithmetic or logical operations. The reason for this is that it is much easier to design a microprocessor that can perform operations on a number contained within one of its own registers than it would be to design one that could perform work on numbers in memory.

8
Loads, Stores,
And Transfers

Beginning with this chapter, the 6502 instruction set will be discussed in detail. The following instructions will be examined in this chapter:

- LDA — Loads accumulator from memory. This transfers the contents of a memory location to the 6502's accumulator register (see Figure 8-1).
- LDX — Loads the X register with the contents of a specified memory location. Similar to LDA, this operates on the X register.
- LDY — Loads the Y register with the contents of a specified memory location.
- STA — Stores accumulator in memory. This transfers the contents of the 6502's accumulator register into a specified byte of memory (see Figure 8-2).
- STX — Stores the value in the X register into a specified memory location. This works like STA, but operates using the X register (see Figure 8-3).
- STY — Stores the value in the Y register into a specified memory location (see Figure 8-4).
- TAX — Transfers the contents of the accumulator to the X register (see Figure 8-5).
- TXA — Transfers the contents of the X register to the accumulator (see Figure 8-6).
- TAY — Transfers the contents of the accumulator to the Y register (see Figure 8-7).
- TYA — Transfers the contents of the Y register to the accumulator (see Figure 8-8).

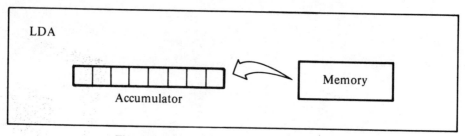

Figure 8-1. Load accumulator from memory

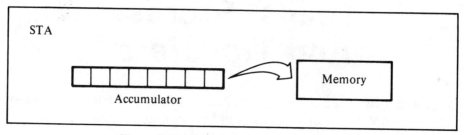

Figure 8-2. Store accumulator in memory

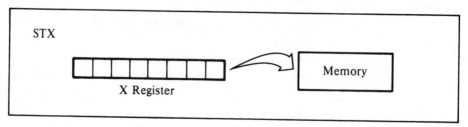

Figure 8-3. Store X register in memory

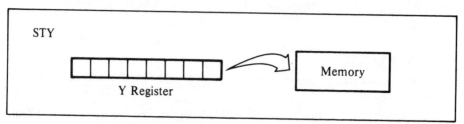

Figure 8-4. Store Y register in memory

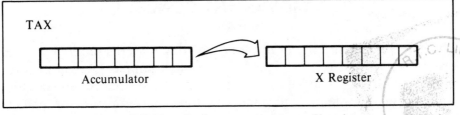

Figure 8-5. Transfer from accumulator to X register

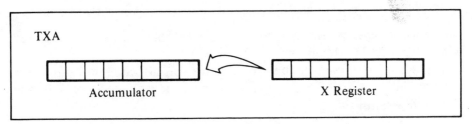

Figure 8-6. Transfer from X register to accumulator

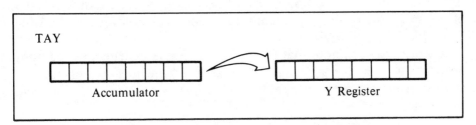

Figure 8-7. Transfer from accumulator to Y register

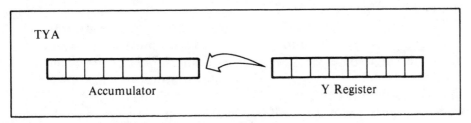

Figure 8-8. Transfer from Y register to accumulator

THE MOVEMENT CONCEPT

To better understand the principles of moving material to implement a load, store, or transfer, consider the following example. Look at the two move operations for the accumulator, or A register. LDA will take the contents of any memory location and transfer them into the 6502's accumulator register. Its assembly form is

```
10          LDA     $300     ;LOAD ACCUMULATOR FROM $300
```
or
```
20          LDA     VALUE    ;LOAD ACCUMULATOR FROM "VALUE"
```

assuming, of course, that a label VALUE had been previously defined with an EQUATE statement.

The value contained in the accumulator can also be stored into any location in memory. To do this, use the mnemonic STA, as in the following examples:

```
30          STA     $300     ;STORE ACCUMULATOR IN $300
40          STA     VALUE    ;STORE ACCUMULATOR IN "VALUE"
```

In the first case, the instruction will store the contents of the accumulator into memory location $300. In the second, it will store the contents of the accumulator into the memory location previously given the label VALUE.

It is important to note that 6502 memory move instructions are non-destructive (that is, the original contents of the location or register moved from are not changed by a move). Consider the following instruction:

```
50     STA  $300
```

Not only would the contents of the accumulator be stored in memory location $300, but the accumulator itself would not be changed. So, if the contents of the accumulator were $FF before the move, they would still be $FF after the move.

Try a sample subroutine using two instructions you already know and one new one. This subroutine, when called from a BASIC program, will print the single-byte value stored in location 775 (decimal) in hexadecimal notation. It uses another monitor subroutine, called PRBYTE, that will output the contents of the accumulator in hex. It will not print a carriage return afterward, so if one is desired it will have to be done in BASIC.

```
 1   ;************************
 2   ; SUBROUTINE TO PRINT A
 3   ; BYTE IN HEX
 4   ;************************
 5   ;
 6              ORG    $300      ;ADDRESS TO BEGIN PROGRAM EXECUTION
 7              OBJ    $800      ;LOCATION TO STORE PROGRAM DURING ASSY
 8   ;
 9   VALUE      EQU    $307
10   PRBYTE     EQU    $FDDA
11   ;
12   PRHEX      LDA    VALUE     ;LOAD ACCUMULATOR WITH VALUE
13              JSR    PRBYTE    ;AND PRINT IT IN HEX
14              RTS              ;THEN RETURN
15              END
```

ASSEMBLED PROGRAM:

**END OF PASS 1
**END OF PASS 2

```
0800        1   ;************************
0800        2   ; SUBROUTINE TO PRINT A
0800        3   ; BYTE IN HEX
0800        4   ;************************
0800        5   ;
0300        6              ORG    $300      ;ADDRESS TO BEGIN PROG. EXECUTION
0300        7              OBJ    $OBJ      ;LOC. TO STORE PROG. DURING ASSY
0300        8   ;
0300        9   VALUE      EQU    $307
0300       10   PRBYTE     EQU    $FDDA
0300       11   ;
0300 AD0703 12   PRHEX      LDA    VALUE  ;LOAD ACCUMULATOR WITH VALUE
0303 20DAFD 13              JSR    PRBYTE ;AND PRINT IT IN HEX
0306 60     14              RTS           ;THEN RETURN
           15              END
```

***** END OF ASSEMBLY

```
          ************************
          * SYMBOL TABLE -- V 1.5 *
          ************************
```

LABEL. LOC. LABEL. LOC. LABEL. LOC.

ZERO PAGE VARIABLES:

** ABSOLUTE VARIABLES/LABELS

VALUE 0307 PRBYTE FDDA PRHEX 0300

SYMBOL TABLE STARTING ADDRESS:6000
SYMBOL TABLE LENGTH:002A

To use the routine from BASIC, first BLOAD the program at $300 (768 decimal). Then, in BASIC, use the form

```
100  POKE  775,A  :REM POKE VALUE TO BE CONVERTED
110  CALL  768    :REM CALL YOUR ROUTINE (AT $300) TO PRINT VALUE
                        IN HEX
120  PRINT        :REM THEN PRINT CARRIAGE RETURN
```

Try entering and assembling this subroutine. It could prove useful in your own BASIC programs.

The remaining eight instructions operate on the same principles as LDA and STA. The mnemonic for each instruction indicates the specific action it performs.

SAMPLE ROUTINE

The following example routine is similar to the one in the previous section, but this one will print out any two-byte value in hex. Store the two bytes in locations 781 ($30D) and 782 ($30E) before calling the routine. Remember to store the low-order byte in 781 and the high-order byte in 782, since that is the order in which the 6502 will look for the address.

```
 1   ;************************
 2   ;* SUBROUTINE TO OUTPUT   *
 3   ;* ANY TWO-BYTE QUANTITY *
 4   ;* IN HEXADECIMAL          *
 5   ;************************
 6   ;
 7   ;
 8            ORG   $300
 9            OBJ   $800
10   ;
11   ;
12   VALL     EQU   $30D
13   VALH     EQU   $30E
14   PRNTYX   EQU   $F940
15   CROUT    EQU   $FD8E
16   ;
17   ;
18   HEXOUT   LDX   VALL      ;LOAD X WITH LOW-ORDER BYTE
19            LDY   VALH      ;LOAD Y WITH HIGH-ORDER BYTE
20            JSR   PRNTYX    ;OUTPUT AS HEX
21            JSR   CROUT     ;THEN DO A CARRIAGE RETURN
22            RTS             ;AND RETURN
23   END      END

ASSEMBLED ROUTINE:

**END OF PASS 1
**END OF PASS 2

0800          1   ;************************
0800          2   ;* SUBROUTINE TO OUTPUT   *
0800          3   ;* ANY TWO-BYTE QUANTITY *
0800          4   ;* IN HEXADECIMAL          *
0800          5   ;************************
0800          6   ;
0800          7   ;
0300          8            ORG   $300
0300          9            OBJ   $800
```

```
0300          10  ;
0300          11  ;
0300          12  VALL     EQU  $30D
0300          13  VALH     EQU  $30E
0300          14  PRNTYX   EQU  $F940
0300          15  CROUT    EQU  $FD8E
0300          16  ;
0300          17  ;
0300 AE0D03   18  HEXOUT   LDX  VALL    ;LOAD X WITH LOW-ORDER BYTE
0303 AC0E03   19           LDY  VALH    ;LOAD Y WITH HIGH-ORDER BYTE
0306 2040F9   20           JSR  PRNTYX  ;OUTPUT AS HEX
0309 208EFD   21           JSR  CROUT   ;THEN DO A CARRIAGE RETURN
030C 60       22           RTS          ;AND RETURN
              23  END      END
***** END OF ASSEMBLY

         **************************
         * SYMBOL TABLE -- V 1.5 *
         **************************

LABEL. LOC. LABEL. LOC. LABEL. LOC.

ZERO PAGE VARIABLES:

** ABSOLUTE VARIABLES/LABELS

VALL   030D   VALH   030E   PRNTYX F940 CROUT FD8E HEXOUT 0300 END 030D

SYMBOL TABLE STARTING ADDRESS:6000
SYMBOL TABLE LENGTH:0042
```

Here is how to use the program from BASIC. Assume the value to be printed in hex is in the BASIC variable V. Note that it is necessary to BLOAD the object program at $300 (decimal 768) before using it from BASIC.

```
100 POKE 782, INT ( V / 256 )

110 REM POKE HIGH BYTE OF VARIABLE V

120 POKE 781, V - INT (,V / 256 ) * 256

130 REM POKE LOW BYTE OF VARIABLE V

140 CALL 768

150 REM PRINT IN HEX
```

Once again, this assembly language subroutine uses subroutines that already exist in the Apple II's F8 monitor ROM. The subroutine labeled CROUT at $FD8E simply prints a carriage return character ($8D) when it is called. Another subroutine, PRTYX at $F940, outputs the two-byte value stored in the X and Y registers in hex.

The example subroutine first loads the X and Y registers from the two memory locations where the BASIC calling program left the value to be printed. It then jumps to the subroutine that outputs the value in hex, and upon return, jumps to the subroutine that RETURNs. This shows why it is necessary to be able to load (and store) the X and Y registers, as well as the accumulator.

9
Simple Arithmetic Operations

The following instructions will be discussed in this chapter:

- INC — Increments (adds 1 to) the quantity in a specified memory location (see Figure 9-1).
- INX — Increments the quantity in the X register (see Figure 9-2).
- INY — Increments the quantity in the Y register (see Figure 9-3).
- DEC — Decrements (subtracts 1 from) the quantity of a specified memory location (see Figure 9-4).
- DEX — Decrements the quantity in the X register (see Figure 9-5).
- DEY — Decrements the quantity in the Y register (see Figure 9-6).
- CLC — Clears the value of the Carry flag, making it 0 (see Figure 9-7).
- SEC — Sets the value of the Carry flag and makes it 1 (see Figure 9-8).
- ADC — Adds the contents of the accumulator to the value contained in a specified memory location, then adds the value of the Carry flag to that, and leaves the result in the accumulator (see Figure 9-9).
- SBC — Subtracts the contents of a specified memory location from the value contained in the accumulator, then subtracts 1 from that; adds the value of the Carry flag to the result, putting the entire calculation back into the accumulator (see Figure 9-10).

In operation, all decrement instructions are similar, as are all increment instructions. Consequently, only four new instruction types — increment, decrement, add, and subtract — are being discussed here.

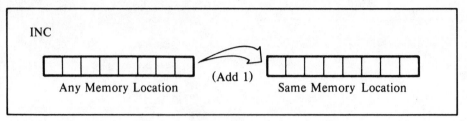

Figure 9-1. Increment memory quantity

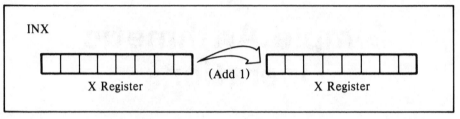

Figure 9-2. Increment X register quantity

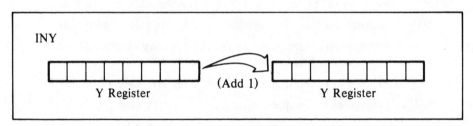

Figure 9-3. Increment Y register quantity

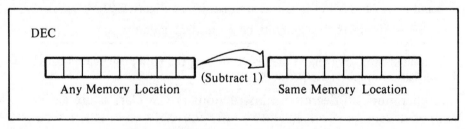

Figure 9-4. Decrement memory quantity

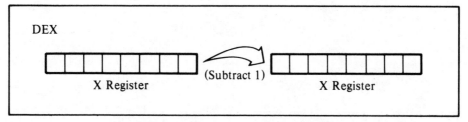

Figure 9-5. Decrement X register quantity

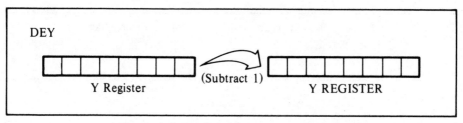

Figure 9-6. Decrement Y register quantity

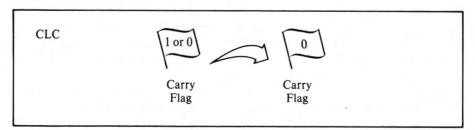

Figure 9-7. Clear Carry flag

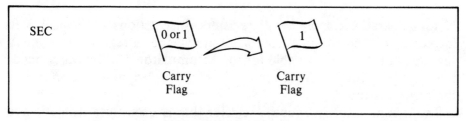

Figure 9-8. Set Carry Flag

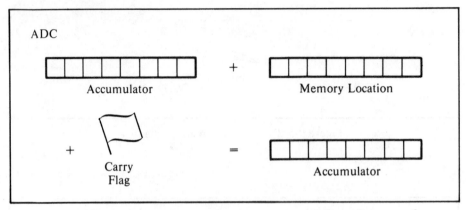

Figure 9-9. Add accumulator, memory, and Carry flag

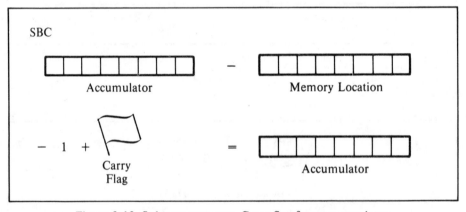

Figure 9-10. Subtract memory, Carry flag from accumulator

INCREMENTING AND DECREMENTING

Not all operations apply to all registers. Instructions are available to increment or decrement memory locations, the X register, and the Y register, but none is available for the accumulator. On the other hand, both of the arithmetic operations shown (add and subtract) interact with the accumulator.

The accumulator is a special register that is used for arithmetic and logical operations. Although it is not given a letter name, it is often referred to as the A register. Since designing a microprocessor with registers that can perform arithmetic and logical operations is an involved task, the designers of the 6502 opted to have only one arithmetic register — the accumulator. The other two registers, X and Y, are usually referred to as the "index registers." Although they cannot be used for arithmetic operations, they work well as incrementing registers and in loops — the assembly language equivalent of the BASIC "FOR...NEXT" function.

Up to now, only instructions that involve either the contents of memory locations or the contents of registers have been discussed. There are, however, other operators to be considered when dealing with microprocessors — flags. Simply stated, a flag is similar to a register in that it is a part of the microprocessor. However, unlike registers, which are eight bits long, flags only have one bit. Therefore, they can only contain either a 1 or a 0.

The 6502 has seven flags that are used for different purposes. These are the Carry flag, Zero flag, Interrupt Disable flag, Decimal flag, Break flag, Overflow flag, and the Sign flag (see Figure 9-11). All can be set or cleared by the 6502 as the result of some operation, and they all reside in a single register known as the "processor status" or "P" register. Some, such as the Carry flag, can be set or cleared with specific instructions. Two instructions for the Carry flag appear in the list of instructions at the beginning of the chapter, CLC (clear the carry) and SEC (set

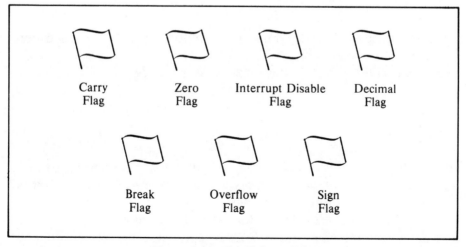

Figure 9-11. Flags of the 6502

the carry). (Note that in computer terms, "clear" usually means to make something 0, and "set" usually means to make something 1.)

ADDITION

In decimal arithmetic, adding two single-digit numbers is simple, as long as the result is a single-digit number. However, if the result of adding two single-digit numbers yields a value that cannot be represented in a single digit, the simplicity disappears. To understand what takes place during the addition of two single-digit numbers that yield a two-digit answer, look at the following example.

First, add 6 and 6. The single-digit answer to the problem is 2. Assuming that using another digit is not allowed, this would be the final answer. In traditional math, however, the process of adding the two 6s together generates a carry. The single-digit answer may be 2, but a 1 is also generated.

Now add the second column. Since, in this example, the carry is only in the second column, the effect is to add a 1 and a 0:

```
 (1)
  0 6
+0 6
-----
  1 2
```

Thus, the answer is 12.

Consider adding 29 and 9. First, perform the low-order digit addition. The result of the addition of a 9 and a 9 is an 8, but a carry is also generated. Next, add the high-order digits with the carry.

```
 (1)
  2 9
+0 9
-----
  3 8
```

The result of the addition for the high-order digits in the second column is 2, plus the carry (1), which equals 3. Note that only a 1 can be carried because no combination of single-digit values yields a carry greater than 1. Consequently, a carry during the addition of any two digits may be considered a conditional function, since in effect, the Carry is either set (equal to 1) or cleared (equal to 0).

Binary Addition

This process ties in with the binary math the 6502 normally works with. The 6502 is an 8-bit microprocessor, and as such, can deal directly with any quantity that can be represented in eight bits. This will be any decimal value from 0 to 255.

Values greater than 255, however, are frequently used with computers. The computer interprets numbers more than eight bits long the same way humans deal with numbers more than one digit long. Humans add another digit, while the computer adds another byte.

When adding two single-digit numbers with a single-digit sum, nothing is carried. Likewise, when the 6502 adds two single-byte values, no carry is generated if the result can be represented in a single byte. On the other hand, when adding two single-byte values, the result of which is a value that cannot be represented in one byte, the 6502 will leave the one-byte value as the answer, and the Carry flag will be set.

```
       BINARY        HEX     DECIMAL
   0001   0001        $11        17
  +0001   1111        $1F        31
  ─────  ─────        ───        ──
   0011   0000        $30        48
```

CARRY IS CLEARED (0)

Since the result of this single-byte addition is represented in a single byte, the Carry has been cleared, as in the following example:

```
         BINARY          HEX      DECIMAL
     1100    1111        $CF        207
    +1111    0000        $F0        240
    ─────   ─────        ───        ───
 (1) 1011    1111      $(1)6F       447
```

CARRY IS SET (1)

In this example, the sum of the addition could not be represented in one byte, so the one-byte sum was left as the answer and the Carry flag was set.

These examples show that the Carry flag exists in the 6502 to facilitate the use of values that are greater than one byte.

Precision Math

Single-byte math is referred to as "single-precision math" and two-byte math is usually referred to as "double-precision math." Single- and double-precision math are generally used in assembly language programming. If more precision is needed, a different type of representation, called "floating point representation," is generally used.

Consider the following single-byte addition routine:

```
 1   ;---------------------------
 2   ;-                         -
 3   ;-SINGLE PRECISION ADDITION-
 4   ;-                         -
 5   ;---------------------------
 6   ;
 7   ;
 8           ORG   $300
 9           OBJ   $800
10   ;
11   ;
12   VAL1    EQU   $30B
13   VAL2    EQU   $30C
14   SUM     EQU   $30D
15   ;
16   ;
17   ADD     CLC              ;FIRST, CLEAR THE CARRY
18           LDA   VAL1       ;LOAD ACCUMULATOR WITH ONE VALUE
19           ADC   VAL2       ;AND ADD THE OTHER ONE TO IT
20           STA   SUM        ;THEN STORE THE RESULT
21           RTS              ;AND RETURN
22   ;
23   ;
24   END     END
```

Everything in this routine should be straightforward. Notice in particular line 17, the first line of the subroutine. Since the state of the Carry flag is not apparent when calling the routine, always clear the Carry flag before performing any additions. Remember, the value of the Carry flag will be added to the result of any addition.

If, by chance, the Carry was set by something outside of the routine and was not cleared before performing the addition, the answer would be incorrect. Always clear the Carry flag before beginning any additions.

After assembling this routine, BLOAD it into the computer (remember to do this at its original address) and enter the monitor to try it. By placing values into locations $30B and $30C and then calling this routine (300G from the monitor), the single-byte result of that addition will be shown by examining location $30D. Remember that if the result of any addition cannot be represented in eight bits, only the lower eight-bit portion of that answer will be available.

Single-precision additions generally do not make useful subroutines because it takes as much or more code to "set up" and call a single-precision addition as would be required to do one every time it was needed. Multiple-precision additions are another story, however, especially if they are part of a subroutine library containing other arithmetic functions. Consider the following example:

```
 1   ;================================
 2   ;=                              =
 3   ;= DOUBLE PRECISION ADDITION    =
 4   ;= VAL1 + VAL2 = SUM            =
 5   ;=                              =
 6   ;================================
 7   ;
 8   ;
 9              ORG   $300
10              OBJ   $800
11   ;
12   ;
13   VAL1L      EQU   $315
14   VAL1H      EQU   $316
15   VAL2L      EQU   $317
16   VAL2H      EQU   $318
17   SUML       EQU   $319
18   SUMH       EQU   $31A
19   ;
20   ;
21   DPADD      CLC              ;FIRST, CLEAR CARRY FLAG
22              LDA   VAL1L      ;THEN ADD THE TWO LOW
23              ADC   VAL2L      ;ORDER BYTES TOGETHER
24              STA   SUML       ;AND STORE RESULT IN SUML
25              LDA   VAL1H      ;THEN ADD HIGH ORDER BYTES WITH
26              ADC   VAL2H      ;CARRY FROM LOW ORDER ADDITION
27              STA   SUMH       ;STORE RESULT IN SUMH
28              RTS              ;THEN RETURN
29   ;
30   ;
31   END        END
```

A double-precision addition is virtually the same as two single-precision additions, but with one important difference. In a double-precision addition, the Carry is not cleared before the high-order bytes are added together. The reason for this is the previous low-order byte addition might have left the Carry flag set, indicating that the result could not be represented in only one byte. Since the value of the carry is always included in additions, it would be added to the sum of the high-order addition.

Before proceeding to subtraction, consider a review of the ADC instruction. The accumulator is loaded with a value. Then the value of a specified memory location is added to the value contained in the accumulator. The value of the Carry flag (either 1 or 0) is added to that, and the resulting eight-bit sum is left in the accumulator. If the sum can be represented in a single byte, the Carry flag is cleared. If not, the Carry flag is set for use by a possible ''next-precision'' addition.

SUBTRACTION

Assuming negative numbers do not exist, consider subtracting 8 from 17. First, find out if the subtrahend is less than or equal to the number from which it is being subtracted. If that is the case, subtract and proceed to the next digit. If that is not the case (as in this example) borrow 1 from the next column. This, of course, decrements the next column, but creates the condition required to do a normal subtraction in the first column.

```
 17           0 (1)7
 -8    =     -0   8
             ─────
              0   9
```

The 6502, on the other hand, will perform this subtraction in a different manner. First, the value of a specified memory location is subtracted from the contents of the accumulator by a process called two's complement addition. If the subtraction causes a borrow, the Carry flag (in this case used as a ''Borrow flag'') is cleared. If no borrow was required, the Carry flag is set.

It is easier to design hardware that will add two values than it is to design hardware that subtracts, even if you must design hardware to complement a binary value (that is, to replace all of its 1s with 0s and all of its 0s with 1s) to make it work. These two processes are used by the 6502 to perform two's complement addition or, in effect, a subtraction.

Consider the following example to see how the 6502 performs subtraction using two's complement addition.

Subtract the following two values:

```
255   OR   $FF   OR    1111  1111
- 2        -$02       -0000  0010
```

Assume the Carry flag was set prior to this subtraction. The state of the Carry flag is indicated with parentheses to the left of the values in the following example.

```
(1)  255   OR  (1)  $FF  OR  (1)  1111   1111
     -2            -$02           -0000   0010
```

The first step in two's complement addition is to take the complement of the value to be subtracted. In binary, the complement of a value is formed by inverting the value of each bit in the number. Thus, each bit that was a 1 is converted to a 0, and vice versa. Now the subtraction looks like the following:

```
(1)  255   OR   (1)  $FF   OR   (1)  1111  1111
     253             $FD             1111  1101
```

The value of the carry is added to the value to be subtracted, as in the following:

```
( )  255   OR   ( )  $FF   OR   ( )  1111  1111
     254             $FE             1111  1110
```

Finally, the two values are added together. As with any addition, if the sum is too large to be represented in eight bits, the Carry is set, as in the following:

```
      255   OR        $FF   OR        1111  1111
     +254            +$FE             1111  1110
(1)   253   (1)      $FD    (1)       1111  1101
```

Remember, before performing a simple subtraction or before the first (lowest order) step in a multiple-precision subtraction, set the Carry flag to indicate that no borrow exists.

The references books listed in Appendix B offer more information on two's complement addition.

SAMPLE ROUTINE

Now consider a single-precision subtraction routine in assembly language.

```
**END OF PASS 1
**END OF PASS 2

0800        1  ;@@@@@@@@@@@@@@@@@@@@@@@@@
0800        2  ;@                       @
0800        3  ;@ SINGLE PRECISION      @
0800        4  ;@ SUBTRACTION           @
0800        5  ;@ VAL1 - VAL2 = RESULT  @
0800        6  ;@                       @
0800        7  ;@@@@@@@@@@@@@@@@@@@@@@@@@
```

```
0800        8  ;
0800        9  ;
0300       10          ORG    $300
0300       11          OBJ    $800
0300       12  ;
0300       13  ;
0300       14  VAL1    EQU    $30B
0300       15  VAL2    EQU    $30C
0300       16  RESULT  EQU    $30D
0300       17  ;
0300       18  ;
0300 38    19  SPSUB   SEC              ;ALWAYS SET CARRY FOR SUBTRACT
0301 AD0B03 20          LDA    VAL1     ;LOAD ACCUMULATOR WITH FIRST VALUE
0304 ED0C03 21          SBC    VAL2     ;SUBTRACT SECOND VALUE FROM IT
0307 8D0D02 22          STA    RESULT   ;THEN STORE "RESULT"
030A 60    23          RTS              ;RETURN
030B       24  ;
030B       25  ;
           26  END     END
```

***** END OF ASSEMBLY

```
*************************
*                       *
* SYMBOL TABLE -- V 1.5 *
*                       *
*************************
```

LABEL. LOC. LABEL. LOC. LABEL. LOC.

**ZERO PAGE VARIABLES:

** ABSOLUTE VARIABLES/LABELS

VAL1 030B VAL2 030C RESULT 030D SPSUB 0300 END   030B

SYMBOL TABLE STARTING ADDRESS:6000
SYMBOL TABLE LENGTH:003A

Remember, just as the Carry should be cleared before any addition operation, the Carry should always be set before a subtraction. This subtraction routine can be assembled, BSAVed, and BLOADed, and run from the monitor, just like the single-precision addition routine.

Now consider a double-precision subtraction routine.

```
 1  ;###############################
 2  ;#                             #
 3  ;# DOUBLE PRECISION SUBTRACT   #
 4  ;# VAL1 - VAL2 = ANS           #
 5  ;#                             #
 6  ;###############################
 7  ;
 8  ;
 9          ORG    $300
10          OBJ    $800
11  ;
12  ;
13  VAL1L   EQU    $314
```

```
14   VAL1H    EQU    $315
15   VAL2L    EQU    $316
16   VAL2H    EQU    $317
17   ANSL     EQU    $318
18   ANSH     EQU    $319
19   ;
20   ;
21   DPSUB    SEC                ;ALWAYS SET CARRY FOR SUBTRACTION
22            LDA    VAL1L       ;FIRST, SUBTRACT LOW ORDER BYTES
23            SBC    VAL2L       ;AND STORE LOW
24            STA    ANSL        ;ORDER ANSWER
25            LDA    VAL1H       ;THEN SUBTRACT HIGH ORDER BYTES
26            SBC    VAL2H       ;WITH BORROW FROM LOW ORDER
27            STA    ANSH        ;SUBTRACT. STORE RESULT
28            RTS
29   ;
30   ;
31   END      END
```

Again, similarities exist between the double-precision addition subroutine and this double-precision subtraction subroutine. Notice that the Carry is set only before the first, low-order byte subtraction. That in turn will either clear or set the Carry, depending on whether a borrow was generated or not. The status of the Carry flag then will be taken into account in the high-order subtraction process.

10
Different Addressing Modes

Instructions discussed in this chapter include LDA, LDX, LDY, STA, STX, STY, INC, DEC, ADC, and SBC. All these instructions should be familiar by now. However, in this chapter each will be used with some different "addressing modes."

IMPLIED MODE

Thus far, all instructions discussed use either the IMPLIED addressing mode or the ABSOLUTE addressing mode. Consider the IMPLIED addressing mode first. Instructions such as INX, DEY, RTS, CLC, TXA, and so forth, use the IMPLIED addressing mode. All 6502 instructions do something to something. Generally speaking, the instructions do something to a register, a flag, or a memory location. These instructions use the IMPLIED addressing mode. For example,

- INX — Increment the X register; the object of the instruction is implied by the instruction.
- CLC — Clear the Carry flag; again, the object of the instruction is implied by the instruction.

• RTS — Return from subroutine; once again, the target is implied.

All simple (no operand) 6502 instructions use the IMPLIED addressing mode.

ABSOLUTE MODE

The other mode used thus far is the ABSOLUTE addressing mode. Instructions like LDA, STY, ADC, and so forth, can all use the ABSOLUTE addressing mode. These are all "three-byte" instructions, where the first byte is, of course, the instruction's op-code and the second and third bytes contain an absolute address. Consider the following examples:

• LDA $F0F0 — Load the accumulator with the value contained in the address $F0F0.

• ADC $300 — Add (with carry) the contents of memory location $300 to the accumulator.

The different number of bytes required by an instruction can be determined by looking in the machine code field of the assembly listings. As mentioned before, the two ABSOLUTE address bytes are reversed, with the low-order byte always preceding the high-order byte. This is how the 6502 requires all addresses to be stored. So, a typical assembly line might look like the following: 300: 8C0A03 1 STY $30A. All instructions that load, store, or perform some arithmetic or logical operation may use the ABSOLUTE addressing mode.

IMMEDIATE MODE

It is often useful to load a register with a constant or to add a register with a constant. This is performed using the IMMEDIATE addressing mode. Just as in BASIC, statements such as these might be used:

```
10  A = 45
20  B = 12
30  A = B + 14
40  A = A - 22
```

The same assignments of constants can be done in assembly language. Consider the following examples:

```
1    LDA   #$2D
2    LDY   #OVER
3    LDX   /OVER
4    ADC   #$0C
```

The "#" is used to indicate the Immediate addressing mode in 6502 assembly language. This example would be interpreted as follows:

- LDA #$2D — Load the accumulator with the quantity $2D.

- LDY #OVER — Load the Y register with the value of the label OVER from the assembler's symbol table. (For example, if OVER was defined as $3E, this instruction would load the number $3E into the Y register. If OVER was defined as $C010, only the low-order byte ($10) would be loaded into the Y register.)

- LDX /OVER — The "/" is commonly used to indicate the immediate value of the high-order byte of an address or label. Thus, if the value of OVER was $C010, this line would load the X register with $C0.

- ADC #$0C — Adds the contents of the accumulator with carry, to the constant $0C and leaves the result in the accumulator.

Thus, instructions using the ABSOLUTE addressing mode affect the contents of the byte in memory specified by the operand. IMMEDIATE mode instructions consider the operand to be a constant. Note that only load instructions can use the IMMEDIATE addressing mode. In BASIC the following command is prohibited: 100 1 = A. In assembly language, the following is prohibited: 100 STA #01. In the IMMEDIATE mode, the number 1 (above) is actually the value 1, not a memory location.

The following program performs the function of clearing ONERR...GOTO status in Applesoft and is identical to POKE 216,0 in Applesoft:

```
1    ;*** CLEARS ONERR...GOTO STATUS
2    ;
3            ORG   $300
4            OBJ   $800
5    ;
6    ERRFLG  EPZ   $D8
7    ;
8    CLRERR  LDA   #$0      ;STORE A ZERO IN
9            STA   ERRFLG   ;THE ONERR STATUS FLAG
10           RTS            ;AND RETURN
11           END
```

ASSEMBLED PROGRAM:

```
**END OF PASS 1
**END OF PASS 2

0800         1  ;*** CLEARS ONERR...GOTO STATUS
0800         2  ;
0300         3          ORG  $300
0300         4          OBJ  $800
0300         5  ;
0300         6  ERRFLG  EPZ  $D8
0300         7  ;
0300 A900    8  CLRERR  LDA  #$0      ;STORE A ZERO IN
0302 85D8    9          STA  ERRFLG   ;THE ONERR STATUS FLAG
0304 60     10          RTS           ;AND RETURN
            11          END

***** END OF ASSEMBLY

            *************************
            *                       *
            * SYMBOL TABLE -- V 1.5 *
            *                       *
            *************************

LABEL. LOC.   LABEL. LOC.   LABEL. LOC.

** ZERO PAGE VARIABLES:

ERRFLG 00D8

** ABSOLUTE VARIABLES/LABELS

CLRERR 0300

SYMBOL TABLE STARTING ADDRESS:6000
SYMBOL TABLE LENGTH:0022
```

While assembling this routine, notice the format of line 8, which uses an IMMEDIATE addressing mode instruction. In the machine code field, notice first the op-code for LDA IMMEDIATE ($A9) followed by the immediate value to be loaded, $00.

Look down a line and notice the instruction STA ERRFLG appears to be an ABSOLUTE addressing mode instruction. However, only two bytes are used to represent the line, not the usual three.

ZERO PAGE ADDRESSING

Earlier, Page 0 of memory ($0-$FF) was noted as having special significance to the 6502. One specialty of Page 0 is that is has its own addressing mode called ZERO PAGE addressing mode. ZERO PAGE addressing is very similar to ABSOLUTE addressing. However, since it only takes one byte of memory to specify the ABSOLUTE address of a memory location in ZERO PAGE, only one byte is used. Code can be written exactly as if it were in the ABSOLUTE mode and the assembler itself will determine when to use ZERO PAGE mode. Consider the following lines:

```
1   ZPLOC   EPZ  $4F      ; ZERO PAGE ADDRESS
2   LOC     EQU  $1000    ; ABSOLUTE ADDRESS
3   ;
4           LDA  $00      ; ZERO PAGE ADDRESSING
5           LDX  LOC      ; ABSOLUTE ADDRESSING
6           STY  ZPLOC    ; ZERO PAGE ADDRESSING
7           ADC  $2D      ; ZERO PAGE ADDRESSING
```

Even though lines 4 through 7 look as though they should generate equal amounts of object code when assembled, that is not the case. The lines with Load instructions with ZERO PAGE operands will generate only two bytes of code — one for the instruction and one for the ZERO PAGE address. The other will, of course, generate three bytes — one for the instruction and two for the ABSOLUTE address specified in the operand. Remember, the assembler takes care of all of this.

In actual applications, the ZERO PAGE addressing mode is extremely useful. It allows performing the same function in a third less code than used by ABSOLUTE mode instructions. As an added bonus, ZERO PAGE instructions execute faster than their ABSOLUTE mode counterparts.

The purpose of this procedure is to define locations that will be referenced repeatedly throughout programs as ZERO PAGE locations. This allows saving a byte (and a few microseconds) every time a ZERO PAGE instruction is used where an ABSOLUTE one might have been.

As an example of this, rewrite the double-precision addition routine from the last chapter, using ZERO PAGE variables instead. The original routine took 20 bytes.

```
1   ;===============================
2   ;=                            =
3   ;= DOUBLE PRECISION ADDITION  =
4   ;= VAL1 + VAL2 = SUM          =
5   ;=                            =
6   ;===============================
7   ;
8   ;
9           ORG  $300
10          OBJ  $800
11  ;
12  ;
13  VAL1L   EPZ  $18
14  VAL1H   EPZ  $19
15  VAL2L   EPZ  $1A
16  VAL2H   EPZ  $1B
17  SUML    EPZ  $1C
18  SUMH    EPZ  $1D
19  ;
20  ;
```

```
21  DPADD  CLC              ;CLEAR CARRY FOR ADD
22         LDA   VAL1L      ;ADD LOW ORDER BYTES
23         ADC   VAL2L
24         STA   SUML       ;AND STORE IN LOW SUM
25         LDA   VAL1H      ;THEN ADD HIGH ORDER BYTES
26         ADC   VAL2H
27         STA   SUMH       ;AND STORE IN HIGH ORDER SUM
28         RTS              ;THEN RETURN
29  END    END
```

When entering and assembling this version, note only 14 bytes are required to do the same job.

Reservations on Use of ZERO PAGE

ZERO PAGE addressing is so advantageous in the 6502 that its extensive use makes code written for the 6502 the fastest of any of the 1 MHz microprocessors. Of course, Applesoft BASIC, the Apple monitor, and DOS all use ZERO PAGE heavily because of this. Since, in almost all cases, assembly language programs will be called from BASIC or DOS or both, it is important not to "step on" the important ZERO PAGE locations that Applesoft, the Monitor, and DOS reserve for their own uses. A map of the reserved ZERO PAGE locations appears in the new Apple II reference manual.

To be safe, limit ZERO PAGE use to the locations from $18 to $1F, as these don't appear ever to be used. Of course, when calling a monitor subroutine or something which requires setting up a ZERO PAGE location before entering it, that is entirely different. Problems only arise when you set a location to a certain value and another routine changes that location.

The 6502 has numerous other addressing modes. Others will be discussed later on in the book.

11
Branching and Looping

Instructions to be discussed in this chapter include the following:

- BCC — Branch if Carry flag is cleared. When this instruction is executed, program execution will continue at the address specified if the Carry flag is cleared; if the Carry is set, execution will continue with the next instruction.
- BCS — Branch if Carry flag is set. Branches to specified address only if Carry flag is set; if the Carry is cleared, execution will continue at the next instruction.
- BEQ — Branch on result equal to zero. If the result of the previous operation was zero, this instruction will branch to the specified address. If the result is non-zero, execution will continue with the next instruction.
- BNE — Branch on result not equal to zero. This instruction branches only if the result of the previous instruction is not equal to zero.
- CMP — Compare the specified memory location's contents with the contents of the accumulator. In effect, this instruction does a subtraction (accumulator — memory), but does not affect the contents of either the accumulator or the memory location.
- CPX — The same as CMP, but compares the value of a specified memory location with the X register instead of the accumulator.
- CPY — The same as CMP and CPX, but uses the Y register.
- JMP — Jump to new location. Similar to a GOTO instruction in BASIC,

this instruction jumps to the specified memory location and resumes program execution there.

In BASIC, program conditional branches can be performed using the IF...THEN statement, as in the following:

```
10  IF R = 0 THEN GOTO 40
20  IF R > 0 THEN GOTO 60
```

Similar operations can be performed in assembly language with a series of BRANCH instructions.

LOOP operations are easily performed in BASIC. The most straightforward way to accomplish this is with FOR...NEXT instructions, as in the following:

```
30  FOR N = 1 TO 40
40  PRINT "−";
50  NEXT N
```

No assembly language equivalent exists for the FOR...NEXT loop in BASIC. However, other BASIC instructions can perform the same operation that a FOR...NEXT loop does in BASIC. The following section of code will perform exactly the same as the FOR...NEXT loop previously mentioned:

```
60  N = 1
70  PRINT "−";
80  N = N + 1
90  IF N < 41 THEN GOTO 70
```

Even though no FOR...NEXT equivalent exists in assembly language, other instructions can be used to create assembly language code similar to the BASIC code previously mentioned.

The key instruction type used to perform both conditional branches and loops in assembly language is called the Conditional Branch instruction. Assembly language for the 6502 has a number of branch instructions including BCC, BCS, BEQ, and BNE. Since the Carry flag has been discussed already, the operations of the Branch on Carry clear and Branch on Carry set instructions (BCC, BCS) should be apparent. To understand the Branch on result equal to zero (BEQ) and the Branch on result not equal to zero (BNE) instructions, the Zero flag must be discussed.

THE ZERO FLAG

As mentioned in earlier chapters, the 6502 has six other flags in addition to the Carry flag. One of them is the Zero flag. As previously discussed, the microprocessor itself will set or clear the Carry flag as a result of additions and subtractions. Other instructions will also affect the Carry flag and can be found by checking the table in Appendix F.

All 6502 instructions that change the contents of either a memory location or register will either set or clear the Zero flag, depending on whether the result of that operation was a zero. This can be useful because it means that if the result of an addition, subtraction, increment, or decrement is equal to zero, the Zero flag will be set. If not, it will be cleared.

BRANCHES

The 6502 instruction set contains a number of conditional branch instructions. All of them operate on the status of a flag. For example, when a BEQ is executed, the 6502 will examine the Zero flag. If it is set, indicating that the result of the last operation was zero, the branch will occur. If not, the next instruction will be executed. The following section of code illustrates this:

```
1             LDY   #$2      ;LOAD Y WITH 2
2             DEY            ;NOW IT EQUALS 1
3             BEQ   RETURN   ;IT'S NOT ZERO SO DO NEXT LINE
4             DEY            ;NOW IT EQUALS 0
5             BEQ   RETURN   ;SO BRANCH TO RETURN
6             LDY   #$00     ;THIS LINE WON'T GET EXECUTED
7   RETURN    RTS
```

As mentioned earlier, branch instructions can be used to perform loops. When used with decrement instructions, branches can perform negative loops. Consider the following BASIC code:

```
10 Y = 40
20 PRINT "—";
30 Y = Y − 1
40 IF Y > 0 THEN GOTO 20
50 PRINT
60 RETURN
```

This subroutine will print a border of minus signs across the screen. Now, do exactly the same thing in assembly language, as in the following:

```
 1  ;====================================
 2  ;=                                  =
 3  ;= SUBROUTINE TO PRINT A BORDER     =
 4  ;= OF MINUS SIGNS ACROSS            =
 5  ;= THE APPLE II'S SCREEN            =
 6  ;=                                  =
 7  ;====================================
 8  ;
 9  ;
10            ORG   $300
11            OBJ   $800
12  ;
13  ;
14  CRDO      EQU   $DAFB
15  OUTDO     EQU   $DB5C
16  ;
17  ;
18  BORDER    LDY   #$28      ;DO LOOP $28 (40) TIMES
19  BDR1      LDA   #$2D      ;LOAD A WITH ASCII VALUE OF "-"
20            JSR   OUTDO     ;AND PRINT IT
21            DEY             ;THEN, DECREMENT Y ONCE
22            BNE   BDR1      ;IF IT'S NOT ZERO YET, LOOP
23            JSR   CRDO      ;IF IT IS, DO A CARRIAGE RETURN
24            RTS             ;AND THEN RETURN
25  ;
26  ;
27  END       END
```

ASSEMBLED PROGRAM:
**END OF PASS 1
**END OF PASS 2

```
0800            1  ;====================================
0800            2  ;=                                  =
0800            3  ;= SUBROUTINE TO PRINT A BORDER     =
0800            4  ;= OF MINUS SIGNS ACROSS            =
0800            5  ;= THE APPLE II'S SCREEN            =
0800            6  ;=                                  =
0800            7  ;====================================
0800            8  ;
0800            9  ;
0300           10            ORG   $300
0300           11            OBJ   $800
0300           12  ;
0300           13  ;
0300           14  CRDO      EQU   $DAFB
0300           15  OUTDO     EQU   $DB5C
0300           16  ;
0300           17  ;
0300 A028      18  BORDER    LDY   #$28      ;DO LOOP $28 (40) TIMES
0302 A92D      19  BDR1      LDA   #$2D      ;LOAD A WITH ASCII VALUE OF "-"
0304 205CDB    20            JSR   OUTDO     ;AND PRINT IT
0307 88        21            DEY             ;THEN, DECREMENT Y ONCE
0308 D0F8      22            BNE   BDR1      ;IF IT'S NOT ZERO YET, LOOP
030A 20FBDA    23            JSR   CRDO      ;IF IT IS, DO A CARRIAGE RETURN
030D 60        24            RTS             ;AND THEN RETURN
030E           25  ;
030E           26  ;
               27  END       END
```

```
***** END OF ASSEMBLY

         *************************
         *                       *
         *  SYMBOL TABLE -- V 1.5 *
         *                       *
         *************************

LABEL. LOC.  LABEL. LOC.  LABEL. LOC.

** ZERO PAGE VARIABLES:


** ABSOLUTE VARIABLES/LABELS

CRDO  DAFB  OUTDO  DB5C  BORDER 0300  BDR1  0302  END   030E

SYMBOL TABLE STARTING ADDRESS:6000
SYMBOL TABLE LENGTH:003A
```

Enter this routine, assemble it, and print an assembly listing. Two things are worth noting in this listing. The first is a matter of form or programming style, and the second is the assembly of the branch instruction on line 22.

Labeling

In assembly language, the entry point of a subroutine should have a label that describes the function of the subroutine. In the previous subroutine, the entry point is labeled BORDER since the function of the routine is to print a border of minus signs. Also, note that the routine calls a subroutine labeled OUTDO. This is an Applesoft internal subroutine that prints or outputs the character found in the accumulator when it's called. Its label stands for "output do."

Notice that this subroutine has two labels. The second label is used only as a target for the branch instruction so that the routine will loop the required number of times. This internal or local label is called BDR1. If this routine had two more local labels, they would be labeled BDR2 and BDR3, respectively. This local labeling format is another useful tool in making assembly language programs easy to understand. Labeling entry points to describe the function of a subroutine helps define what that subroutine does. By logically labeling all local labels within a subroutine, it is easier to understand the code involved in that routine. For examples of this, look at the assembly listings of the monitor ROM found in the Apple II reference manual.

Relative Addressing

Look at line 22 of the assembly listing, particularly the machine code field.

```
0308 D0F8    22    BNE BDR1
```

Normally, three bytes of machine code are generated for this instruction — one for the instruction's op-code, and two more for the absolute address to branch to. Instead only two can be found.

Conditional branches in the 6502 instruction set are assembled into two bytes. The first is the instruction op-code. The second byte tells the microprocessor the "offset" from the current code address in memory, to the target of the branch. The eighth (high-order) bit of the offset byte tells the microprocessor which direction to branch.

If the high-order bit is set (that is, the offset value is some number greater than $7F), the branch instruction will branch backward in memory. If it is cleared, it will branch forward. The offset is calculated from the first byte of the instruction immediately following the branch instruction itself. This type of addressing is called "relative addressing" because the target address is some address relative to the present location, plus the specified offset.

As the examples show, to remember these concepts in assembly language, use a line of the following form and allow the assembler to figure out the offset.

```
MNEMONIC                OPERAND
CONDITIONAL BRANCH   ADDRESS OR LABEL
```

There is, however, one thing you will have to watch out for. Since the offset is only one byte long, you can only branch to a location that's less than 256 bytes away from the location of the branch instruction. What this means is that you can branch 127 bytes forward from the instruction following a branch, or 128 bytes backward from that point. Since most 6502 instructions are between two and three bytes long, this means that you can usually branch to a label about 50 lines away.

If you attempt to assemble a program which contains a branch that is farther away than allowed, an assembly time "branch out of range error" will occur. If this occurs, the code will have to be modified so the long branch doesn't happen. This is usually done by using the branch instruction's complement and an ABSOLUTE jump (JMP) instruction. For example,

```
10 RT2      LDY COUNT

11          BEQ RT15

12          STY VALUE
```

```
100 RT15    JSR SUB

101         LDA #$1
```

Assuming that the address of the instruction on line 12 (the instruction following the branch) is greater than 127 bytes away from the address of the label RT15, an attempt to assemble this code will result in a branch out of range error. Modifying the code will solve this, as in the following:

```
10 RT2      LDY COUNT

11          BNE RT3

12          JMP RT15

13 RT3      STY VALUE
```

```
100 RT15    JSR  SUB

            LDA #$1
```

The complement instruction of BEQ (BNE, for branch if not equal to zero) is used to branch around the JMP instruction to the continuation of the code. This is a short branch and will be legal. Then use a JMP instruction to the desired location, since jump instructions use absolute addressing and therefore are not restricted to a 255-byte range.

The following are some BASIC examples of the same structure:

```
100 Y = CT

110 IF Y = 0 THEN GOTO 1000

120 VL = Y
```

```
1000 GOSUB 2000

1010 A = 1
```

Logically, this code performs the same function:

```
100 Y = CT
110 IF Y <> 0 THEN GOTO 130
120 GOTO 1000
130 VL = Y
```

```
1000 GOSUB 2000
1010 A = 1
```

Of course, in BASIC there would be no need for the second format, because the IF...THEN...GOTO can branch to any line in a BASIC program.

COMPARES

Compare instructions compare two values — one in a register and one in memory. They behave just like a subtract instruction, except that they don't modify either the register or the memory location involved. Instead, they set or clear certain flags as a result of the subtraction. A typical compare statement might look like this:

```
1       CMP VALUE       ;COMPARE THE CONTENTS OF
                        ;ACCUMULATOR WITH THE
                        ;CONTENTS OF THE LOCATION
                        ;"VALUE", AND SET FLAGS
```

When this instruction is executed, the Carry flag is set for the subtract. The value in the specified memory location is subtracted from the value in the accumulator. As a result of the subtract, both the Carry and the Zero flags are affected. If the result is zero, then the Zero flag is set. If it's not, it's cleared. If the value in the accumulator is less than that in the memory location, a borrow will be required, so the Carry flag will be cleared. If it's not, the Carry flag is set. The result of the subtraction will be lost after the operation and will not be stored in the accumulator. Therefore, the contents of the accumulator will not be affected by the compare.

Remember that in both 6502 compare instructions and subtract instructions, the form of the operation is

ACCUMULATOR — MEMORY

Consider the following results of a compare instruction in a table:

- IF A = M THEN ZERO FLAG SET
- IF A <> M THEN ZERO FLAG CLEARED
- IF A < M THEN CARRY FLAG CLEARED
- IF A => M THEN CARRY FLAG SET

There are three compare instructions (one for each register), and they all behave exactly the same. The only difference is the registers that are being compared.

- CMP = A − M
- CPX = X − M
- CPY = Y − M

Print Program

Consider the operation of the compare instruction in another real program. This one will print a specified ASCII character up to 255 times. It can be used to print different character borders, feed paper to a printer, or force scrolling by printing repeated carriage returns. To use it, put the ASCII value of the character you want repeated in location 24 ($18). Put the number of times you want the character repeated into location 25 ($19). Then, call the routine.

```
 1   ;********************************
 2   ;*                              *
 3   ;* THIS SUBROUTINE WILL OUTPUT  *
 4   ;* ANY ASCII CHARACTER UP TO    *
 5   ;* 255 TIMES.                   *
 6   ;*                              *
 7   ;********************************
 8   ;
 9   ;
10            ORG $300
11            OBJ $800
12   ;
13   ;
14   CHAR     EPZ $18
15   NUM      EPZ $19
16   OUTDO    EQU $DB5C
17   ;
18   ;
19   REPEAT   LDY  #$0      ;INITIALIZE COUNT IN Y
20   REP1     INY           ;INCREMENT COUNT IN Y
21            LDA  CHAR      ;LOAD THE ACCUMULATOR WITH THE
22            JSR  OUTDO     ;CHARACTER AND OUTPUT IT
23            CPY  NUM       ;ARE WE DONE OUTPUTTING?
24            BNE  REP1      ;IF NOT, CONTINUE OUTPUTTING
25            RTS            ;ELSE, RETURN
26   ;
27   ;
28   END      END
```

```
ASSEMBLED PROGRAM:
**END OF PASS 1
**END OF PASS 2

0800               1  ;*******************************
0800               2  ;*                             *
0800               3  ;* THIS SUBROUTINE WILL OUTPUT *
0800               4  ;* ANY ASCII CHARACTER UP TO   *
0800               5  ;* 255 TIMES.                  *
0800               6  ;*                             *
0800               7  ;*******************************
0800               8  ;
0800               9  ;
0300              10           ORG    $300
0300              11           OBJ    $800
0300              12  ;
0300              13  ;
0300              14  CHAR     EPZ    $18
0300              15  NUM      EPZ    $19
0300              16  OUTDO    EQU    $DB5C
0300              17  ;
0300              18  ;
0300 A000         19  REPEAT   LDY    #$0     ;INITIALIZE COUNT IN Y
0302 C8           20  REP1     INY            ;INCREMENT COUNT IN Y
0303 A518         21           LDA    CHAR    ;LOAD THE ACCUMULATOR WITH THE
0305 205CDB       22           JSR    OUTDO   ;CHARACTER AND OUTPUT IT
0308 C419         23           CPY    NUM     ;ARE WE DONE OUTPUTTING?
030A D0F6         24           BNE    REP1    ;IF NOT, CONTINUE OUTPUTTING
030C 60           25           RTS            ;ELSE, RETURN
030D              26  ;
030D              27  ;
                  28  END      END

****** END OF ASSEMBLY

               *************************
               *                       *
               * SYMBOL TABLE -- V 1.5 *
               *                       *
               *************************

LABEL. LOC.  LABEL. LOC.  LABEL. LOC.

** ZERO PAGE VARIABLES:

CHAR   0018  NUM     0019

** ABSOLUTE VARIABLES/LABELS

OUTDO  DB5C  REPEAT 0300  REP1   0302  END    030D

SYMBOL TABLE STARTING ADDRESS:6000
SYMBOL TABLE LENGTH:0042
```

Each time this routine outputs the specified character, it checks to see if it has been output the specified number of times. If it hasn't, the branch in line 24 directs execution back, and the count is incremented. Then, the whole operation begins again.

The following is an example of how to use this routine from BASIC. It will print a border of 40 minus signs across the screen.

```
100 REM SUBROUTINE TO PRINT A BORDER OF —"S
110 POKE 24, ASC (" — ")
120 POKE 25, 40
130 CALL 768
140 RETURN
```

Clearing Graphics

Another sample subroutine will clear the LORES graphics screen to any color, and erase the bottom four lines of text. Normally, if a GR from BASIC is used, the screen is cleared to black, and the bottom four lines are erased. This routine performs similar functions, but allows picking the color to which the screen is cleared. A couple of subroutines form the Monitor ROM again. They are

- SETGR $FB40 — Sets the Apple to the LORES graphics mode with four lines of text. Clears the screen to black. Same as BASIC command GR.

- VLINE $F828 — Similar to BASIC instruction of same name. Plots a LORES graphics line in the current color from A through value in $2D at Y.

- SETCOL $F864 — Sets the LORES color to the number found in A. Similar to the BASIC instruction COLOR=.

```
 1   ;*****************************
 2   ;*                          *
 3   ;* CLEARS LORES GRAPHICS    *
 4   ;* SCREEN TO SPECIFIED COLOR *
 5   ;*                          *
 6   ;*****************************
 7   ;
 8   ;
 9            ORG   $300
10            OBJ   $800
11   ;
12   ;
13   CLRCOL  EPZ   $18
14   V2      EPZ   $2D
15   VLINE   EQU   $F828
16   SETCOL  EQU   $F864
17   SETGR   EQU   $FB40
18   ;
19   ;
20   COLOR   JSR   SETGR    ;SET LORES GRAPHICS MODE
21           LDA   CLRCOL   ;THEN SET COLOR TO
22           JSR   SETCOL   ;COLOR SPECIFIED
23           LDA   #$27     ;NOW SET LENGTH OF VLINE
24           STA   V2
25           LDY   #$0      ;INITIALIZE COUNT IN Y
26   COL1    LDA   #$0      ;SET TOP-OF-LINE POSITION
27           JSR   VLINE    ;AND DRAW ONE LINE AT CURRENT
28           INY            ;Y COLUMN. INCREMENT Y.
29           CPY   #$28     ;SCREEN DONE?
30           BNE   COL1     ;NO, DO NEXT COLUMN
```

```
                 31            RTS            ;YES, RETURN
                 32  ;
                 33  ;
                 34  END       END
```

ASSEMBLED PROGRAM:

**END OF PASS 1
**END OF PASS 2

```
0800              1  ;******************************
0800              2  ;*                            *
0800              3  ;*  CLEARS LORES GRAPHICS     *
0800              4  ;*  SCREEN TO SPECIFIED COLOR *
0800              5  ;*                            *
0800              6  ;******************************
0800              7  ;
0800              8  ;
0300              9            ORG   $300
0300             10            OBJ   $800
0300             11  ;
0300             12  ;
0300             13  CLRCOL    EPZ   $18
0300             14  V2        EPZ   $2D
0300             15  VLINE     EQU   $F828
0300             16  SETCOL    EQU   $F864
0300             17  SETGR     EQU   $FB40
0300             18  ;
0300             19  ;
0300 2020FB      20  COLOR     JSR   SETGR    ;SET LORES GRAPHICS MODE
0303 A518        21            LDA   CLRCOL   ;THEN SET COLOR TO
0305 2064F8      22            JSR   SETCOL   ;COLOR SPECIFIED
0308 A927        23            LDA   #$27     ;NOW SET LENGTH OF VLINE
030A 852D        24            STA   V2
030C A000        25            LDY   #$0      ;INITIALIZE COUNT IN Y
030E A900        26  COL1      LDA   #$0      ;SET TOP-OF-LINE POSITION
0310 2028F8      27            JSR   VLINE    ;AND DRAW ONE LINE AT CURRENT
0313 C8          28            INY            ;Y COLUMN. INCREMENT Y.
0314 C028        29            CPY   #$28     ;SCREEN DONE?
0316 D0F6        30            BNE   COL1     ;NO, DO NEXT COLUMN
0318 60          31            RTS            ;YES, RETURN
0319             32  ;
0319             33  ;
                 34  END       END
```

****** END OF ASSEMBLY

```
                 *************************
                 *                       *
                 *  SYMBOL TABLE -- V 1.5 *
                 *                       *
                 *************************
```

LABEL. LOC.   LABEL. LOC.   LABEL. LOC.

** ZERO PAGE VARIABLES:

CLRCOL 0018   V2   002D

** ABSOLUTE VARIABLES/LABELS

This program draws a full deflection VLINE at each column on the screen. To use it from BASIC, POKE into location 24 ($18) the number of the color the screen is to clear to, and call the routine at 768 ($300).

The BASIC equivalent for this is the following:

```
100 REM SUBROUTINE TO CLEAR LORES SCREEN TO ANY COLOR
110 GR
120 COLOR = C
130 FOR Y = 0 TO 39
140 VLINE 0, 39 AT Y
150 NEXT Y
160 RETURN
```

They both work the same, of course, only the assembly language version does it much faster.

SUMMARY

Compare instructions perform a single-precision subtraction, but they don't affect the register subtracted from. They set the appropriate flags, relative to the result of the subtraction. Branch instructions will branch program execution to a new location on a condition, the condition always being the state of a certain flag.

All branch instructions use relative addressing, which results in the instruction only requiring two bytes — one op-code, one offset byte. This normally restricts branches to locations less than 50 program lines away from the branch instruction.

12
Indexed Addressing

Instructions and assembler directives introduced in this chapter include the following:

- CMP — Compare the value in the accumulator with the value in a specified memory location (see Figure 12-1).
- CPX — Compare the value in the X register with the value in a specified memory location (see Figure 12-2).
- ASC — ASCII string. The assembly language equivalent of a string DATA statement in BASIC, this allows assembly language storage of a specified ASCII string in memory.

As discussed in an earlier chapter, the X and Y registers are generally referred to as index registers because they are used in the INDEXED

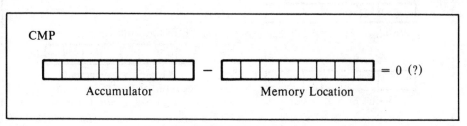

Figure 12-1. Compare

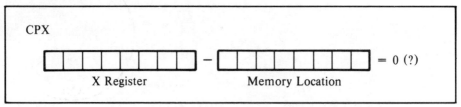

Figure 12-2. Compare X register with memory

ADDRESSING mode. This addressing mode, which can be used with several of the instructions already discussed, is very useful for performing sequential retrieval of data and run-time specification of values. Consider the following example:

    1   LDA COUNT

When this instruction is executed, the accumulator will be loaded with the value stored in the memory location that has the label COUNT. In the INDEXED addressing mode, however, data can be specified to come from the address of the label plus the positive offset found in one of the index registers. Consider the same instruction, this time in the INDEXED BY X addressing mode instead of the ABSOLUTE mode.

    1   LDA COUNT,X

This instruction reads, "Load the accumulator with the value found at the address COUNT plus the value in the X register" (see Figure 12-3). Thus, the address from which the data will be loaded will depend on the value in the X register at the time this instruction is executed. If the X register contains a 0 when the instruction is executed, then the instruction will load the accumulator with data from the address

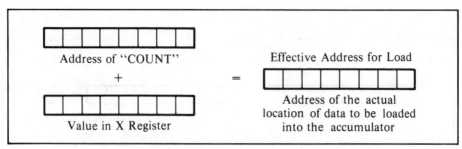

Figure 12-3. Load accumulator plus X register

COUNT. If, however, the X register contains the value $FF, the accumulator will be loaded with the value found in location COUNT + $FF. The following example shows this operation:

```
1        LDA $1000     ;LOADS FROM ADDRESS $1000
2        LDY #$50
3        LDA $1000,Y    ;LOADS FROM ADDRESS $1050
4        LDY #$F0
5        LDA $1000,Y    ;LOADS FROM ADDRESS $10F0
6        LDX #$2E
7        LDA LABEL,X    ;LOADS FROM ADDRESS LABEL+$2E
```

To use the INDEXED addressing mode, enter code using the format shown. In the operand field the address or label should appear, followed by a comma, followed by the letter of the index register to be used. To find out if the instruction desired may be used with INDEXED addressing, see the 6502 instruction set table in Appendix F. Don't put any spaces in the operand field, since most assemblers assume this means the ABSOLUTE mode is being requested.

THE ASC DIRECTIVE

Basically, two types of things can be found in any assembly listing: actual 6502 instructions that will be assembled into machine code, and assembler directives that are used only by the assembler itself. One of these assembler directives allows putting ASCII string data directly into memory, and is very similar to the DATA statement in BASIC.

To include a string "HELLO" in a program, for example, use statement of the form

```
1  HELLO$ ASC "HELLO"
```

During assembly, the assembler would put the ASCII value for each of the characters in the string into sequential memory locations. Since these bytes cannot be executed by the 6502, it's important never to let the program try to execute them.

This is the key difference between assembly language data statements and BASIC's DATA statement. In BASIC, the program will "skip over" all DATA statements at execution time. In assembly language, the programmer is responsible for making sure that the data statements will not be executed. For this reason, they are usually gathered together, either at the beginning (before the entry location) or at the end (after the RTS) of the subroutine that will use them.

The following sample program makes use of the ASCII string data assembler directive, as well as INDEXED addressing. It is used to print the word "--ERROR--", but could be used to print any phrase, as long as it is less than 255 characters long. To do so, insert the desired string into the operand field of the ASC directive, then make the CPX instruction's operand the immediate number of characters in your string.

```
 1    ;****************************
 2    ;*                          *
 3    ;* ERROR MESSAGE PRINTING    *
 4    ;* SUBROUTINE                *
 5    ;*                          *
 6    ;****************************
 7    ;
 8    ;
 9            ORG    $300
10            OBJ    $800
11    ;
12    ;
13    OUTDO   EQU    $DB5C
14    ;
15    ;
16    ERPRNT  LDX    #$0       ;INITIALIZE COUNT IN X
17    ERP1    LDA    ERR$,X    ;FETCH ONE CHARACTER FROM
18            JSR    OUTDO     ;STRING AND OUTPUT IT.
19            INX              ;INCREMENT X (THIS POINTS
                                   TO THE NEXT CHARACTER)
20            CPX    #$9       ;COMPARE X TO 9 (THE NUMBER
                                   CHARACTERS IN MESSAGE)
21            BNE    ERP1      ;NO CONTINUE OUTPUTTING
22            RTS              ;YES, RETURN
23    ERR$    ASC    '--ERROR--'
24    ;
25    ;
26    END     END
```

ASSEMBLED LISTING:

```
**END OF PASS 1
**END OF PASS 2

0800          1    ;****************************
0800          2    ;*                          *
0800          3    ;* ERROR MESSAGE PRINTING    *
0800          4    ;* SUBROUTINE                *
0800          5    ;*                          *
0800          6    ;****************************
0800          7    ;
0800          8    ;
0300          9            ORG $300
0300         10            OBJ $800
0300         11    ;
0300         12    ;
0300         13    OUTDO   EQU $DB5C
0300         14    ;
0300         15    ;
0300 A200    16    ERPRNT  LDX   #$0       ;INITIALIZE COUNT IN X
0302 BD0E03  17    ERP1    LDA   ERR$,X    ;FETCH ONE CHARACTER FROM
0305 205CDB  18            JSR   OUTDO     ;STRING AND OUTPUT IT.
0308 E8      19            INX             ;POINT TO THE NEXT CHARACTER
0309 E009    20            CPX   #$9       ;IS STRING DONE?
030B D0F5    21            BNE   ERP1      ;NO CONTINUE OUTPUTTING
030D 60      22            RTS             ;YES, RETURN
```

```
030E 2D2D45    23 ERR$      ASC '--ERROR--'
0311 52524F
0314 522D2D
0317           24 ;
0317           25 ;
               26 END       END

***** END OF ASSEMBLY

               *************************
               *                       *
               * SYMBOL TABLE -- V 1.5 *
               *                       *
               *************************

LABEL. LOC.  LABEL. LOC.  LABEL. LOC.

** ZERO PAGE VARIABLES:


** ABSOLUTE VARIABLES/LABELS

OUTDO DB5C  ERPRNT 0300  ERP1   0302  ERR$   030E  END   0317

SYMBOL TABLE STARTING ADDRESS:6000
SYMBOL TABLE LENGTH:003A
```

This program also uses the Applesoft internal routine OUTDO to output ASCII characters. Applesoft must be the current language in the machine when attempting to run this routine.

Type in and assemble this program. You'll find a sizable number of hex values in the machine code field on line 23. These are the ASCII values for each of the characters in the string. All the values will probably not fit on that line, so they'll be continued on the next line.

When the program is first entered, the first character of the string will be printed. This is because the X register will have a 0 in it and the indexed LDA instruction will just take the character found at the label ERR$. Each time the loop is done, however, the X index register will be incremented. This will cause the LDA to pick up the next character in the string each time it is executed.

INDIRECT INDEXED ADDRESSING

Operation of the normal INDEXED addressing mode is fairly straightforward. There is another addressing mode, INDIRECT INDEXED, which, although not quite as simple, offers versatility to the indexed addressing concept. Consider the one limitation of regular INDEXED addressing as discussed so far. At the time of assembly, the base address of the index operation must be specified. During program execution, up to 255 bytes can be indexed forward of the base address. Suppose you wanted to print a message that was longer than 256 bytes.

The INDIRECT INDEXED mode of addressing can solve some of these problems by allowing you to index virtually anywhere in memory. In the operand field, specify the address of a memory location in ZERO PAGE. When the instruction is executed, it will take (as the base address) the address pointed to by the values in that ZERO PAGE memory location and the next one. In addition, the value of the Y register will be added to form the effective address of the operation. An example might help explain this operation.

```
1   ADRL    EPZ     $18
2   ADRH    EPZ     $19
3
4           LDA     #$00
5           STA     ADRL
6           LDA     #$F0
7           STA     ADRH
8           LDY     #$01
9           LDA     (ADRL),Y
```

In lines 1 and 2, two consecutive ZERO PAGE locations are labeled. In lines 4 through 7 the address $F000 is stored. Remember, the 6502 will access all addresses low-order byte first, so the $00 is in the first byte (ADRL) and the $F0 is in the second byte (ADRH). Thus, the base address is $F000. But since this instruction is also indexed by the Y register, it will add the value of the Y register to the base address to get the actual address. In this example, the Y register contains $01, so the address from which data will be loaded in line 9 is going to be $F001 (see Figure 12-4).

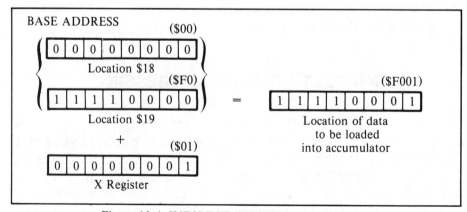

Figure 12-4. INDIRECT INDEXED addressing mode

INDIRECT INDEXED is a very powerful addressing mode. Not only does it allow indexing into any memory location, but it also manages to do that using only two bytes — one for the op-code and the other for the address of the first ZERO PAGE location of the pointer.

The following program will turn on the Apple II's high-resolution graphics mode and clear the screen to black. However, unlike the HGR or HGR2 commands available in BASIC, this routine uses the INDIRECT INDEXED addressing mode to store 0s in all of the memory locations of the selected screen. This results in a virtually instant screen clear, compared to BASIC's rather slow dissolve.

```
 1    ;****************************
 2    ;*                          *
 3    ;* FAST HIRES SCREEN CLEAR  *
 4    ;* FOR EITHER HIRES PAGE    *
 5    ;*                          *
 6    ;****************************
 7    ;
 8    ;
 9            ORG    $300
10            OBJ    $800
11    ;
12    ;
13    ADRL    EPZ    $18
14    ADRH    EPZ    $19
15    COLOR   EPZ    $30
16    HPAG    EPZ    $E6
17    SCALE   EPZ    $E7
18    ROT     EPZ    $F9
19    ;
20    GRAPSW  EQU    $C050
21    FULLSW  EQU    $C052
22    MIXSW   EQU    $C053
23    SCR1SW  EQU    $C054
24    SCR2SW  EQU    $C055
25    HIRESW  EQU    $C057
26    ;
27    ;
28    CLRSC1  LDA    SCR1SW    ;SCREEN #1 ENTRY POINT
29            LDA    MIXSW     ;SET FOR MIXED TEXT/GRAPHICS
30            LDA    #$20      ;$20= HIGH ORDER ADDRESS, SCREEN #1
31            JMP    CLR1
32    CLRSC2  LDA    SCR2SW    ;SCREEN #2 ENTRY POINT
33            LDA    FULLSW    ;SET FOR FULL SCREEN GRAPHICS
34            LDA    #$40      ;$40= HIGH ORDER ADDRESS, SCREEN #2
35    CLR1    STA    HPAG      ;SAVE IN HIRES "PAGE" BYTE
36            STA    ADRH      ;AND IN HIGH ORDER ADDRESS
37            LDA    HIRESW    ;THEN SET HIRES SWITCH
38            LDA    GRAPSW    ;AND GRAPHICS SWITCH
39            LDA    #$1       ;SET SCALE = 1
40            STA    SCALE
41            LDA    #$0       ;AND ROT=0
42            STA    ROT
43            STA    COLOR     ;COLOR=0, TOO
44            STA    ADRL      ;AS DOES LOW ORDER ADDRESS
45            CLC              ;NOW, CALCULATE THE HIGH ORDER
46            LDA    HPAG      ;BYTE OF THE ADDRESS OF
47            ADC    #$20      ;THE END OF THE SCREEN
```

```
48              TAX            ;AND SAVE IN X
49              LDA   COLOR    ;COLOR=0 (BLACK)
50    CLR2      LDY   #$0      ;INITIALIZE Y TO CLEAR
51    CLR3      STA   (ADRL),Y ;SIX ROWS OF SCREEN.
52              INY
53              BNE   CLR3
54              INC   ADRH     ;NEXT SIX ROWS
55              CPX   ADRH     ;SCREEN DONE YET:
56              BNE   CLR2     ;NO, CONTINUE
57              RTS            ;YES, RETURN
58    ;
59    ;
60              END
```

ASSEMBLED PROGRAM:

```
**END OF PASS 1
**END OF PASS 2

0800            1   ;*****************************
0800            2   ;*                           *
0800            3   ;* FAST HIRES SCREEN CLEAR   *
0800            4   ;* FOR EITHER HIRES PAGE     *
0800            5   ;*                           *
0800            6   ;*****************************
0800            7   ;
0800            8   ;
0300            9             ORG   $300
0300           10             OBJ   $800
0300           11   ;
0300           12   ;
0300           13   ADRL      EPZ   $18
0300           14   ADRH      EPZ   $19
0300           15   COLOR     EPZ   $30
0300           16   HPAG      EPZ   $E6
0300           17   SCALE     EPZ   $E7
0300           18   ROT       EPZ   $F9
0300           19   ;
0300           20   GRAPSW    EQU   $C050
0300           21   FULLSW    EQU   $C052
0300           22   MIXSW     EQU   $C053
0300           23   SCR1SW    EQU   $C054
0300           24   SCR2SW    EQU   $C055
0300           25   HIRESW    EQU   $C057
0300           26   ;
0300           27   ;
0300 AD54C0    28   CLRSC1    LDA   SCR1SW   ;SCREEN #1 ENTRY POINT
0303 AD53C0    29             LDA   MIXSW    ;SET FOR MIXED TEXT/GRAPHICS
0306 A920      30             LDA   #$20     ;$20= HIGH ORDER ADDRESS,
                                                 SCREEN #10
0308 4C1303    31             JMP   CLR1
030B AD55C0    32   CLRSC2    LDA   SCR2SW   ;SCREEN #2 ENTRY POINT
030E AD52C0    33             LDA   FULLSW   ;SET FOR FULL SCREEN GRAPHICS
0311 A940      34             LDA   #$40     ;$40= HIGH ORDER ADDRESS,
                                                 SCREEN #2
0313 85E6      35   CLR1      STA   HPAG     ;SAVE IN HIRES "PAGE" BYTE
0315 8519      36             STA   ADRH     ;AND IN HIGH ORDER ADDRESS
0317 AD57C0    37             LDA   HIRESW   ;THEN SET HIRES SWITCH
031A AD50C0    38             LDA   GRAPSW   ;AND GRAPHICS SWITCH
031D A901      39             LDA   #$1      ;SET SCALE = 1
031F 85E7      40             STA   SCALE
0321 A900      41             LDA   #$0      ;AND ROT=0
0323 85F9      42             STA   ROT
```

```
0325 8530      43              STA   COLOR      ;COLOR=0, TOO
0327 8518      44              STA   ADRL       ;AS DOES LOW ORDER ADDRESS
0329 18        45              CLC              ;NOW, CALCULATE THE HIGH ORDER
032A A5E6      46              LDA   HPAG       ;BYTE OF THE ADDRESS OF
032C 6920      47              ADC   #$20       ;THE END OF THE SCREEN
032E AA        48              TAX              ;AND SAVE IN X
032F A530      49              LDA   COLOR      ;COLOR=0 (BLACK)
0331 A000      50    CLR2      LDY   #$0        ;INITIALIZE Y TO CLEAR
0333 9118      51    CLR3      STA   (ADRL),Y   ;SIX ROWS OF SCREEN.
0335 C8        52              INY
0336 D0FB      53              BNE   CLR3
0338 E619      54              INC   ADRH       ;NEXT SIX ROWS
033A E419      55              CPX   ADRH       ;SCREEN DONE YET:
033C D0F3      56              BNE   CLR2       ;NO, CONTINUE
033E 60        57              RTS              ;YES, RETURN
033F           58     ;
033F           59     ;
               60              END
```

***** END OF ASSEMBLY

```
    *************************
    *                       *
    * SYMBOL TABLE -- V 1.5 *
    *                       *
    *************************
```

LABEL. LOC.   LABEL. LOC.   LABEL. LOC.

** ZERO PAGE VARIABLES:

ADRL 0018 ADRH 0019 COLOR 0030 HPAG 00E6 SCALE 00E7 ROT 00F9

** ABSOLUTE VARIABLES/LABELS

```
GRAPSW C050   FULLSW C052   MIXSW  C053
SCR1SW C054   SCR2SW C055   HIRESW C057
CLRSC1 0300   CLRSC2 030B   CLR1   0313
CLR2   0331   CLR3   0333   END    03FF
```

SYMBOL TABLE STARTING ADDRESS:6000
SYMBOL TABLE LENGTH:00A2

This routine actually does more than merely clear the screen. This should give some idea of just what goes into a seemingly simple BASIC instruction like HGR. The part of this program that demonstrates the use of the INDIRECT INDEXED addressing mode is in the last nine lines of the program. Essentially, the goal here is to fill the entire range of memory from $2000-$3FFF (for HIRES Page 1) or $4000-$5FFF (for Page 2) with 0s.

Suppose the goal is to clear HIRES Page 1 (that is, store a 0 in every byte from $2000-$3FFF). Store a pointer to the first byte of the screen, $2000, in the two ZERO PAGE memory locations labeled ADRL,H. Then load the accumulator with a 0. Store the value 0 in all memory locations in the accumulator that can possibly be indexed into using the Y register (locations $2000-$20FF). Afterward, increment the value in ADRH. It was formerly $20, and is $21 after the increment, so now the pointer in ADRL,H is at $2100. Repeat this process until the entire screen memory is filled with 0s.

ENTRY POINTS

As well as demonstrating INDIRECT INDEXED addressing, the previous routine has a structural feature that has not yet been discussed — two different entry points. In assembly language programming, as in BASIC programming, it is common to use different entry points to a routine. This allows the combination of two or more relatively similar operations in the same routine. In the sample routine, entering at location CLRSC1 will set HIRES screen 1 and clear it. Entering the routine at CLRSC2 will set HIRES screen 2 and clear it.

INDEXED INDIRECT MODE

One other INDEXED addressing mode that the 6502 can use is the INDEXED INDIRECT addressing mode. It is seldom used in 6502 assembly language programming on the Apple II because it uses up a lot of valuable ZERO PAGE memory.

In the INDIRECT INDEXED addressing mode, the effective address of the instruction is created by the address contained in the ZERO PAGE location specified in the operand and next location, plus the value of the Y register. In comparison, instructions using INDEXED INDIRECT addressing load (or store) values from (or to) the address contained in a pair of ZERO PAGE locations which are derived as the sum of a base ZERO PAGE operand address plus the value in the X register. An example of INDEXED INDIRECT addressing is

```
1       LDA     #$FF
2       STA     $03
3       STA     $04
4       LDX     #$03
5       LDA     ($00,X)
```

Lines 1 through 3 store an address ($FFFF) in ZERO PAGE locations $03 and $04. These locations now "point" to address $FFFF. In line 4, the X register is set to a value of 3, and in line 5 the accumulator is loaded from the memory location pointed to by the ZERO PAGE locations at the base address ($0) plus the value of the X register (3). As this is address $3 (which, along with the next location, points to address

$FFFF), the accumulator is loaded with the current value of location $FFFF.

SUMMARY

INDEXED addressing mode can usually use either the X or the Y register. Instructions are of the form

    MNEMONIC ADDRESS,REGISTER

For example,

    LDA LABEL,X

In this mode, the value of the index register is added to the operand address to form the actual address for the instruction. INDIRECT INDEXED addressing uses the Y index register only. Instructions are of the form

    MNEMONIC (ZERO PAGE address), Y

For example,

    LDA (LABEL), Y

The INDEXED INDIRECT addressing mode is seldom used in 6502 assembly language programs for the Apple II. Just so you may recognize it, instructions are of the form

    MNEMONIC (ZERO PAGE address, X)

For example,

    LDA (LABEL, X)

13
Equivalent Values
And the Negative Flag

Instructions discussed in this chapter include the following:

- BPL — Branch on result plus. Branches to the specified address if the Negative flag is cleared; otherwise continues program execution with the next statement.
- BMI — Branch on result minus. The complement to BPL; branches only if the Negative flag is set.

In assembly language, a single byte may represent any integer in the range 0 to 255 or it may represent any integer in the range −128 to +127. When expressing integers, Applesoft treats both positive integers or their negative equivalents identically, since they are actually the same number. Thus, in Applesoft, the following two instructions are equivalent:

```
10  CALL -151   : REM GOTO MONITOR
20  CALL 65385 : REM GOTO MONITOR
```

Both of these call the Apple Monitor entry point at $FF69. The two values −151 and 65385 are both equivalent to $FF69.

Signed single-byte arithmetic is rarely used in assembly language programming, but knowledge of the structure of signed values can be very useful since it incorporates the use of the Negative flag.

The Negative flag works just like all the other 6502 flags. Certain internal operations will either set or clear it, depending on the sign of the result. Some of the operations that affect the Negative flag are add, subtract, compare, load, increment, decrement, and transfer operations. Any operation that affects the Zero flag also will affect the Negative flag.

For the purpose of identification, the 6502 considers any number to be negative if the high-order bit is set. This means any single-byte value greater than $7F (127) is considered negative. To expand this definition, if the result of any internal operation is a value greater than $7F, the Negative flag will be set. If the value is $7F or less, the Negative flag will be cleared.

This feature is particularly good for index operations that use decrementing loops, provided the index is not initialized to some value greater than $80. For example

```
1              LDY    #$09      ;INITIALIZED COUNT
2      LOOP    LDA    DATA,Y    ;GET DATA FOR SUBROUTINE
3              JSR    SUBRTN    ;DO SUBROUTINE
4              DEY              ;DECREMENT COUNT
5              BPL    LOOP      ;IF Y<$FF THEN LOOP
6              RTS              ;ELSE, RETURN
```

In this subroutine, the value of the index Y will be decremented and the loop will be performed as long as the value of Y is not negative (it will not be negative if it is 9, 8, 7, 6, 5, 4, 3, 2, 1, or 0). But when it is decremented again, Y will have a value of $FF which, having its high-order bit set, is a negative value. The Negative flag will, of course, be set by this operation, so the branch will not occur.

The same function could have been performed using a compare (CPY) instruction. However, it would have taken longer to execute the same code, and it would have taken up more space.

14
Logic Functions

Instructions in this chapter include the following:

- AND — Logically AND the value in the accumulator and a value in a specified memory location, leaving the result in the accumulator.

- ASL — Arithmetic shift left. Shifts all bits in a byte (either accumulator or memory) once to the left, thus leaving a 0 in the lowest order bit, and moving the value from the highest order bit into the Carry (see Figure 14-1).

- EOR — Exclusive OR memory and accumulator. Logically Exclusive ORs the value in the accumulator and that in a specified memory location, leaving the result in the accumulator.

- LSR — Logical shift right. Complement to ASL; shifts all bits in a byte (either accumulator or memory) once to the right, thus leaving the low-order bit in the Carry, and a 0 in the high-order bit (see Figure 14-2).

- ORA — OR accumulator and memory. Logically OR the accumulator and a specified memory location, leaving the result in the accumulator.

- ROL — Rotate left (accumulator or memory). Rotates all bits to the left, through the Carry; similar to ASL, but the value in the Carry before the operation is not lost, but is instead moved into the lowest order bit (see Figure 14-3).

- ROR — Rotate right. Complement to ROL; performs a similar operation, but rotates to the right (see Figure 14-4).

Logical operations are used to manipulate the bits in a byte. Move and transfer operations just move entire bytes from one place to another.

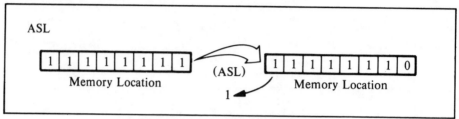

Figure 14-1. Arithmetic shift left

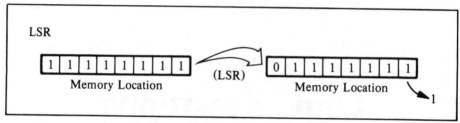

Figure 14-2. Logical shift right

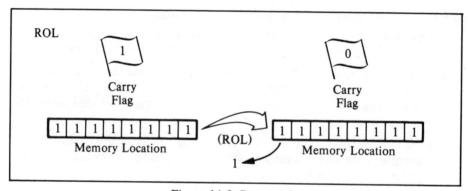

Figure 14-3. Rotate left

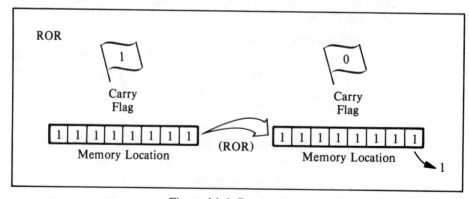

Figure 14-4. Rotate right

Arithmetic operations treat all bytes as representing an arithmetic value. Logical operations treat bytes as representing a series of bits. Classical hardware models, as well as BASIC examples, will be used in describing the operation of logical instructions.

AND, OR, AND EOR

The primary unit of digital electronics is the "logic gate." Simply put, this is a device with two inputs and one output. The binary state of the output will depend only on the binary states of the inputs. One type of logic gate is the AND gate. The electronic schematic for the AND gate is

Since this is a binary device, the inputs can be in one of two states: 0 or 1. The output can be in only one of these states as well. Simply stated, an AND gate works as follows: if input A is equal to 1, and input B is equal to 1, then the output equals 1.

In BASIC, this could be stated as

```
10   C=0
20   IF A=1 AND B=1 THEN C=1
```

The output will be 1 only if both inputs are 1. Otherwise, the output will be 0. In the 6502 instruction set, the AND operation will perform logical ANDs on every bit in the accumulator with their positional equivalent bits on a byte in memory. This could be illustrated as in Table 14-1.

First, the lowest order bits are ANDed together. In this example, both are 0, so the result is 0, and the next higher bits are ANDed. Here each is 1 so the result is 1. This same process occurs for the rest of the

Table 14-1. AND Operation

		Binary		Hex	Decimal
Accumulator	=	1100	1010	$CA	202
Memory Location	=	1001	1110	$9E	158
AND		1000	1010	$8A	138

bits in the accumulator and memory byte. The result of the entire operation is left in the accumulator.

Another type of logic function is the OR. Its electronic schematic is

Input (A) ——⊃ Output (C)
Input (B) ——

If input A equals 1 or input B equals 1, then the output equals 1. This condition is also true if both inputs equal 1. In fact, the only time the output will equal 0 is when both inputs equal 0. We could construct the following similar structure in BASIC:

```
20  C=0
30  IF A=1 OR B=1 THEN C=1
```

The assembly language instruction which ORs two values together is ORA, which ORs the value in the accumulator with a value in memory (see Table 14-2).

Starting with the lowest order bits, OR each bit pair together. In this example, all but the high-order bit pair has at least one bit equal to 1, so all of the resultant bits are set to 1. As with the AND operation, the result of the OR operation is left in the accumulator.

The last of the logical operations involving both the accumulator and memory is the Exclusive OR. Its electronic schematic is

Input (A) ——⊃ Output (C)
Input (B) ——

Although BASIC does not have an EOR function specifically, it can be represented by the following:

```
10  C=0
20  IF A<>B THEN C=1
```

Table 14-2. OR Operation

		Binary		Hex	Decimal
Accumulator	=	0011	1110	$3E	62
Memory Location	=	0111	0011	$73	115
OR		0111	1111	$7F	127

Table 14-3. EOR Operation

		Binary		Hex	Decimal
Accumulator	=	1001	1110	$9E	158
Memory Location	=	1111	0100	$F4	224
EOR	=	0110	1010	$6A	106

Consider the operation outlined in Table 14-3. The Exclusive OR function can be thought of as an inverted compare. That is, when the two inputs are different, the output will be high, and when they are the same, the output will be low.

A variety of different addressing modes is available for these logical operations, including the following examples:

```
 1  SAMPLE AND #$80
 2  AND #VALUE
 3  AND LABEL
 4  AND BUFFER,X
 5  AND (ADRL),Y
 6  ORA #VALUE
 7  ORA /LABEL
 8  ORA (POINTL),Y
 9  ORA LAB
10  EOR #COLOR
11  EOR BUFFER,Y
```

Remember, all of these operations leave the result in the accumulator and affect both the Zero flag and the Negative flag. To find all of the addressing modes available, see Appendix F.

SHIFTS AND ROTATES

Shift and rotate operations comprise another type of logical operation available in the 6502 instruction set. They differ from the above operations in that they change either the value in the accumulator or the value of a memory location; their operations never involve both.

To illustrate how a shift operation works, consider Table 14-4. In a left shift, all of the bits in a byte are moved over one position to the left. The "hole" that is left in the space formerly occupied by the lowest order bit is always filled with a 0. The highest order bit is moved into the Carry flag.

Consider Table 14-5. Again, all bits are moved one place to the left, and a 0 is placed in the least significant bit. The most significant bit is shifted into the Carry flag, and the original value of the carry is lost. Each time a value is shifted to the left, that number is in effect multiplied by 2, as long as a 1 bit doesn't get shifted off the end, in which case a carry is generated.

Consider this instruction's complement, LSR, as shown in Table 14-6. In this operation, all bits are shifted once to the right, and a 0 is placed in the high-order bit. The low-order bit is shifted into the Carry flag, and the original value of the carry is lost.

There are also two operations which are similar to shifts, only nothing is lost. Those are the rotate instructions. Instead of setting a bit to 0 and losing one bit, these instructions simply move the bits around in a circle.

Consider the ROR instruction as shown in Table 14-7. In this operation, the carry is moved right, into the high-order bit position. The rest of the value is shifted right, with the lowest bit ending up in the carry. Every time this operation is performed, the bits move one place, but no bits are ever lost. In fact, if this operation were performed nine times, the original value and the original carry would be restored.

The last instruction of the series, ROL, is the complement of ROR, as shown in Table 14-8. Here the carry is shifted into the low-order bit, and the value is shifted left. Once again nothing is lost, so if this operation were performed nine times, the original value and carry would be restored.

Shift and rotate operations are available using a variety of addressing modes, including the ACCUMULATOR mode. To use this addressing mode with the LISA assembler, put the mnemonic in the mnemonic field, but put nothing in the operand field. This is the same method used with IMPLIED addressing instructions.

```
1 LABEL ASL   ; SHIFT ACCUMULATOR LEFT
2       LSR   ; SHIFT ACCUMULATOR RIGHT
3       ROL   ; ROTATE ACCUMULATOR LEFT
4       ROR   ; ROTATE ACCUMULATOR RIGHT
```

NOTE: If an assembler other than the LISA assembler is used, you may have to put the letter "A" in the operand field, to denote the ACCUMULATOR mode. If in doubt, see the assembler's user's manual.

The other addressing modes available for this family of instructions are ZERO PAGE, ZERO PAGE INDEXED BY X, ABSOLUTE, and ABSOLUTE INDEXED BY Y. Typical code might look like the following:

```
1 START ASL VAL
2       LSR ZPVAL
3       ROL ZPVAL,X
4       ROR BUFFER,Y
```

When the instructions discussed in this chapter are used with any of these addressing modes, they affect a byte in memory, not the accumulator.

Table 14-4. Shift Operation

		Binary	Hex	Decimal
Memory Location	=	0000 0001	$01	1
ASL		0000 0010	$02	2

Table 14-5. ASL Operation

		Carry	Binary	Hex	Decimal
Memory Location	=	1	0010 1001	$29	41
ASL		0	0101 0010	$52	82

Table 14-6. LSR Operation

		Carry	Binary	Hex	Decimal
Memory Location	=	0	1100 1001	$C9	201
LSR		1	0110 0100	$64	100

Table 14-7. ROR Operation

		Carry	Binary	Hex	Decimal
Accumulator	=	1	0010 0101	$25	37
ROR		1	1001 0010	$92	146

Table 14-8. ROL Operation

		Carry	Binary		Hex	Decimal
Memory Location	=	1	0010	0010	$22	34
ROL		0	0100	0101	$45	69

APPLICATIONS

Some applications for logical instructions include the following:

- AND — Bit mask testing; testing a value to see if a certain bit is on, and clearing unwanted bits from a byte.

- OR — Testing a value to see if a certain bit is off; setting certain bits in a byte.

- EOR — Complementing a value.

- ASL, LSR — Multiplying or dividing a multiple-precision value by 2; sequential bit tests.

- ROL, ROR — Branching on status of either the high-order bit or the low-order bit, using the carry; sequential bit tests, saving the original value.

15
Debugging Instructions

Instructions discussed in this chapter include the following:

- NOP — No operation. This is the null instruction of the 6502 instruction set; memory, registers, and flags are not affected.
- BRK — Break. Used in debugging; upon executing a break instruction, the 6502 will jump to the address found in locations $FFFE and $FFFF.

The two most commonly used methods of debugging a BASIC program involve either deleting (or remarking over) suspect lines, and the insertion of STOP instructions in the code. The 6502 instruction set contains instructions that allow you to perform similar operations in assembly language. These are the NOP and BRK instructions. Consider the following BASIC code:

```
100 A = B + C
110 GOSUB 2000
120 PRINT AN$
```

If, while debugging, you find that the subroutine at line 2000 is incorrect, the GOSUB instruction could be eliminated and the program run. This is accomplished by typing the line number and running the program. In assembly language, if you suspect some piece of code is causing problems and you want to eliminate it, you must reassemble the program, resave it, reload it, and so forth.

The NOP instruction is useful in cases like these. Consider the following code:

```
300   A502     1   LDA   ADRL
302   205003   2   JSR   SUB1
305   A8       3   TAY
306   8C6D03   4   STY   INDEX
```

Say the JSR instruction in line 2 is causing problems. To eliminate it temporarily, put NOP instructions in each of the three bytes that the JSR instruction now takes. Once this is done, the JSR instruction is effectively removed from the code. The procedure to patch over a section of code is as follows:

1. BLOAD the object code into memory at the address from which it originated.

2. Enter the Apple II's monitor.

3. Disassemble the suspect code with the L monitor command. Using the sample code above, you would type 300L.

4. Look at the disassembly and calculate both the starting address and the number of bytes of the code to be patched over. Write down the values of the bytes to be replaced. If it turns out that something else is causing the problem, you'll want to be able to restore those bytes without reloading the object file.

5. Using the monitor's STORE IN MEMORY command, replace all bytes in the suspect code with the value $EA. This is the op-code value for the 6502's NOP instruction. In the previous example, type 302: EA EA EA.

6. Finally, disassemble the code again, to make sure that only the code desired was patched over with no-ops. Then, run the code using the G monitor command.

If all of this was done using the example, the new disassembly of the object code would look like the following:

```
0300:   A502     LDA   $02
0302:   EA       NOP
0303:   EA       NOP
0304:   EA       NOP
0305:   A8       TAY
0306:   8C6D03   STY   $36D
```

Another useful debugging instruction is the BRK instruction. With it, you can perform the same kind of assembly language code debugging as you could in BASIC using the STOP command. When BASIC interprets a STOP command, it halts program execution and prints the line number of the STOP instruction. The BRK instruction in the Apple II does even more to help the debugging effort.

When the 6502 executes a BRK instruction, it jumps to the address found in two special locations: $FFFE and $FFFF. These two addresses direct, or vector, program execution to a special BRK instruction handling routine in the Apple II monitor ROM. This routine not only halts program execution, but also prints the location at which that execution stopped and the current value of each of the 6502's registers.

The op-code for the BRK instruction is $00. Break instructions can be patched into code the same way that NOPs are patched. Or, if you are assembling a reasonably long program and are not overly optimistic about its success the first time, break instructions can be put into the source code at regular intervals.

After the code is assembled, and it is time to debug the program, you can run the program and eliminate the BRKs one by one as you verify that a section of code is functioning properly. If you have included the break instructions correctly in the source code, the easiest way to eliminate them is by patching them over, using the techniques described earlier, with NOP instructions. Finally, when the code works, reassemble it without the BRK instructions.

Both BRK and NOP instructions are single-byte instructions with no operands. Since they are often used from the monitor, it would be a good idea to remember their op-codes. Their op-codes are

```
BRK = $00
NOP = $EA
```

When programming, you will find these to be the most useful instructions in the entire 6502 instruction set.

NOTE: For some reason, when using the BRK instruction with the Apple II, the value given for the location at which program execution stopped is 2 more than it should be. This is one of the very few firmware bugs in the Apple II. When using the BRK instruction, remember to subtract 2 from the "stopped at" value given.

16
The Stack

Instructions to be covered in this chapter include the following:

- JSR — Jump to Subroutine. Similar to JMP, but saves a return address on the stack like a GOSUB in BASIC.
- PHA — Push accumulator onto the stack; puts the current value in the accumulator onto the top of the stack (see Figure 16-1).
- PLA — Pull accumulator off the stack. Takes one byte off the top of the stack and stores it in the accumulator (see Figure 16-2).

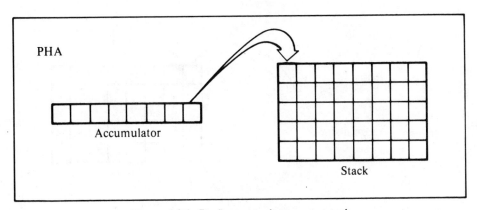

Figure 16-1. Push accumulator onto stack

• RTS — Return from subroutine. Pulls a two-byte address off the stack, and resumes program execution at that address.

The only two places where the 6502 can keep a value are in one of its internal registers or in memory. One area of memory, Page 0, is special because instructions accessing it take up less space and operate faster. Indirect instructions also use ZERO PAGE addresses for their pointers.

Another special area in the 6502's memory is Page 1, which goes from $100 to $1FF. This area is called the "stack." The 6502 instruction set has a number of instructions that use the stack.

ORDER OF THE STACK

The stack (sometimes called a "push-down stack" or "last-in, first-out storage") behaves very much like the apparatus used to store and serve plates in a restaurant. Each time a plate is placed on top, the stack sinks down. When you pull the top plate off the stack, the rest pop up, making the new top plate flush with the top of the apparatus. Only one plate can be pushed onto this stack at a time and only one plate can be removed from the stack at a time. The only access to this stack is from the top. A plate can never be pulled out of the middle or from the bottom. For this reason, the last plate put on the stack is always the first to be pulled off.

The 6502 stack behaves just like the restaurant plate stack, but is a stack of bytes, rather than a stack of plates. Up to 256 bytes may be stored on the 6502 stack.

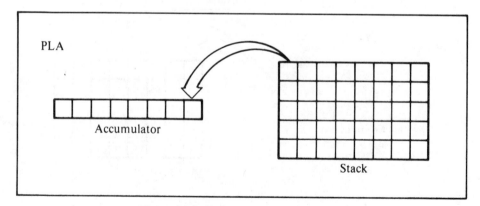

Figure 16-2. Pull accumulator off stack

PHA AND PLA

Two instructions in the 6502 instruction set allow you to push the value in the accumulator onto the stack (PHA) or to pull off the value on the top of the stack (PLA), and then store it in the accumulator. Since they don't affect any addressed memory locations, their addressing mode is IMPLIED. Therefore, they don't require an operand.

```
1      LABEL      PLA        ;PULL ACCUMULATOR FROM STACK
2                 PHA        ;PUSH ACCUMULATOR ONTO STACK
```

These two instructions are suited for temporary storage. To save the value currently in the accumulator, use a temporary memory location as in the following:

```
20     LABEL      STA TEMP   ;SAVE ACCUMULATOR
30                JSR SUB    ;DO SUBROUTINE
40                LDA TEMP   ;RESTORE ACCUMULATOR
```

If the value in the accumulator were saved in a ZERO PAGE location, the entire temporary store-load operation would take four bytes of code. If you were to use the stack for temporary storage, it would only take two bytes of code and would execute faster.

```
50     LABEL      PHA        ;SAVE ACCUMULATOR
51                JSR SUB    ;DO SUBROUTINE
52                PLA        ;RESTORE ACCUMULATOR
```

Temporary saves on the stack have the added advantage of not taking up a lot of valuable ZERO PAGE space. This becomes important when saving more than one byte.

```
23     LABEL      PHA        ;SAVE ACCUMULATOR
24                TXA
25                PHA        ;SAVE X REGISTER
26                TYA
27                PHA        ;SAVE Y REGISTER
28                JSR SUB    ;DO SUBROUTINE
29                PLA
30                TAY        ;RESTORE Y REGISTER
31                PLA
32                TAX        ;RESTORE X REGISTER
33                PLA        ;RESTORE ACCUMULATOR
```

When storing more than one value on the stack, remember the stack is a last-in, first-out device. Therefore, pull off values in the opposite order from which they were pushed on.

JSR AND RTS

The stack is also used by the JSR and RTS instructions. As mentioned earlier, they behave much like their BASIC equivalents, GOSUB and RETURN.

First consider what happens when a JSR instruction is executed. The RETURN address (the address of the next instruction following the JSR in memory) is pushed onto the stack, one byte at a time. Then the 6502 performs a jump to the specified subroutine address.

At the end of the subroutine, the 6502 finds an RTS instruction. When this RTS is executed, two bytes are pulled off the stack, which the 6502 assumes are the current return address for the subroutine. It does a jump to that address, and program execution resumes there. This means that, just as in BASIC, a limited number of subroutines may be nested. In practice, however, that limit is very rarely reached.

By the way, there is no equivalent 6502 assembly language instruction to the BASIC POP instruction. But it can be emulated with two PLA instructions, thus effectively removing the last return address from the stack. Then, the next time an RTS instruction is executed, the previously nested return address will be used.

When using the stack for temporary storage, be careful not to confuse return addresses with data. This could happen if you attempted to push a value on the stack for temporary storage, and then tried to pull it off after entering a subroutine, but before its return. Since the last thing that went on the stack was the return address, you would be attempting to pull the wrong thing. For example:

```
1     LABEL     PHA
2               JSR SUB
```

At this point, the top of the stack would look like the following:

```
RETURN ADDRESS (HIGH-ORDER BYTE)
RETURN ADDRESS (LOW-ORDER BYTE)
DATA FROM ACCUMULATOR
```

Attempting to pull the accumulator off the stack now would yield one of the return address bytes instead, since that's what's on the top of the stack. To keep things straight, just remember to both push and pull the same number of bytes within any one subroutine. Also keep in mind that both the JSR and the RTS instructions use the stack and will affect its contents.

NOTE: Because of the way the 6502 performs a return, the actual value of the return address pushed onto the stack by a JSR instruction is the address of the instruction following the JSR instruction, minus 1.

A
Instructions Not Covered
In this Book

A few 6502 instructions were not described in detail in this book and don't belong to any family of instructions. Because of the construction of the Apple II, including hardware, firmware, and available peripherals, certain instructions are rarely used. These instructions will be briefly discussed in this appendix.

- BIT — Test bits in memory. The BIT instruction behaves exactly like the AND instruction, except that result of the logical AND is not stored in the accumulator. As previously discussed, the AND instruction performs a logical AND on each bit of the value in the accumulator with each bit of the value in a specified memory location. The resulting value is stored in the accumulator. The BIT instruction does all of this, too, only the result is not stored in the accumulator or anywhere else.

  Whenever any logical or arithmetic operation occurs in the 6502, various flags are set or cleared, depending on the value of the result of the operation. These flags may be tested and subsequent operations performed, depending on their states. The Minus, Overflow, and Zero flags are all affected by this instruction.

- BVS — Branch on overflow set. When this branch instruction is encountered, a branch to the specified location will occur if the Overflow flag is set. Otherwise, execution will continue with the next instruction. The Overflow flag is the sixth bit (second MSB) of the status register. All logical and arithmetic instructions affect the Overflow flag. If the result of any logical or arithmetic operation has a 1 in the sixth bit, the Overflow flag will be set by the operation. Conversely, if the result has a 0 in the sixth bit, the Overflow flag will be cleared.

· BVC — Branch on Overflow flag cleared. This is the complement instruction to BVS. When a BVC is encountered, if the Overflow flag is cleared, a branch will occur to the specified location. If it is set, program execution will continue with the next instruction.

· CLD — Clear decimal mode. Sets up the 6502 to do normal binary arithmetic. The 6502 is capable of performing arithmetic operations on two types of values: binary bytes and bytes of BCD (binary-coded decimal) digits. The Apple II never uses the BCD mode. All of its math is done in binary. However, if the 6502 were to be used in processes requiring large amounts of decimal (fixed-point) processing, the decimal mode might be selected. In this mode, all bytes are considered to be two BCD digits, each with an arithmetic range of 0 to 9. Thus, in the decimal mode, a single byte may represent any arithmetic value in the range 0 to 99. Once again, this mode is not used in any of the Apple II's internal software or firmware.

· CLI — Clear interrupt disable flag. Allows the 6502 to accept hardware interrupts. The 6502 chip has a pin on it that an external device requiring immediate attention can pull down. This is the IRQ (interrupt request) pin. There are times, however, when a running program may want to ignore (disable) interrupts for a while. This usually occurs in sections of code where time is critical. In these cases, interrupts may be disabled using the SEI instruction (see below). When interrupts are to be allowed again, the CLI instruction is issued and interrupt processing is performed normally.

The Apple II system does not use interrupts for any of its own applications. However, peripheral cards which plug into the Apple may generate interrupts. For this reason, Apple DOS disables interrupts whenever a disk operation is to occur (disk operations are time-critical), and reenables them when the disk operation is over.

· CLV — Clear Overflow flag. Sets the value of the Overflow flag (the sixth bit of the status register) to 0.

· JMP (indirect) — Jump to new location. Continues program execution at the address specified by the value contained in the operand address and the next one in memory. This instruction allows a program to dynamically alter the target address of a jump instruction. Addressing is similar to indirect addressing used in other instructions. For example

```
LDA #00
STA PTR
LDA #01
STA PTR+1
JMP (PTR)
```

When executed, this code would effect a jump to location $100.

- PHP — Push processor status on stack. Pushes the values of the status register, which contains all of the flags, onto the stack. Sometimes it is convenient to save the current status so that it can be used later. This occurs frequently when a series of logical or arithmetic operations occurs, and a conditional branch will occur as a result of the first one. Consider the following code:

```
LDA #0
AND #0
```

Eventually a branch will be desired as the result of this operation, but more operations are desired first. As the next operation might affect the status flags, the current status can be saved and other operations performed.

```
PHP
ORA THIS
EOR THAT
```

Finally, the original status can be restored with a PLP instruction and a branch performed.

```
PLP
BEQ THERE
```

Processor status is also saved and restored during certain debugging operations and during interrupt processing.

- PLP — Pull processor status from the stack. This is the complementary instruction to PHP. Restores processor status register (flags) from the stack.
- RTI — Return from interrupt. As mentioned in the discussion of the CLI instruction, the 6502 may be interrupted by an external hardware device. If an interrupt does occur, program execution is transferred to an interrupt vector (a special place in memory that holds the address of the code to execute on an interrupt). This code, called an "interrupt handler," must end with an RTI instruction. This instruction will restore the original status of the 6502 (before the interrupt) and return control to the program that was interrupted. As mentioned, interrupts are not used by any of the Apple's internal firmware or software.
- SED — Set decimal mode. Initializes the 6502 to perform arithmetic operations on BCD values. See CLD for more information.
- SEI — Set interrupt disable status. Disables the 6502 from being interrupted via the IRQ pin. For more details, see the CLI instruction.
- TSX — Transfer the value of the stack pointer to the X register. The 6502 stack is actually a page in memory. It resides at memory locations $100-$1FF (Page 1). The stack pointer always specifies or "points out" the byte in Page 1 that is the current "top of stack."

B
Where to Go from Here

Since this book is an introduction to assembly language programming for the Apple II, not all aspects of 6502 programming are covered in detail, and some are not covered at all. The following books are written specifically for the 6502.

6502 Assembly Language

Osborne/McGraw-Hill has two books available on 6502 assembly language including *6502 Assembly Language Programming* by Lance Leventhal and *6502 Assembly Language Subroutines* by Leventhal and Winthrop Saville.

MOS Techology 6500 Programming Manual

This book is from the designers of the 6502. It covers the entire 6500 family and contains programming examples. It is available at most computer stores or from Synertek, Rockwell International, or your Apple dealer.

MOS Technology 6500 Hardware Manual

This book is essential for those planning on building hardware. Available from the same sources as the programming manual.

6502 Software Gourmet Guide and Cookbook

This book is not only an excellent guide to the 6502 instruction set, but also contains several useful, well-written programs and subroutines which can be used right away in your own routines. Written by Robert Findley, the book is available from your computer store or from the publisher:

Scelbi Computer Consulting, Inc.
Elmwood, CT 06110

THE APPLE

Several good sources of assembly language programming information are designed especially for the Apple. If you're serious about Apple programming, join a local Apple user's group. Almost every area of the country has at least one, many of which publish newsletters. Most of these groups also have at least one member who has considerable expertise in assembly language programming. Some groups even have assembly language programming classes.

In addition to joining your local group, consider joining the largest user's group in the world. The Apple Puget Sound Program Library Exchange publishes a ''newsletter'' that is one of the best magazines on Apple around. To join, contact:

A.P.P.L.E.
304 Main Avenue South
Suite O500
Renton, WA 98055
(206) 271-4514

MAGAZINES

Two magazines are very useful to 6502 programmers.

Nibble

This is the best source of information on the Apple, because it's written totally for Apple users. This monthly magazine contains a wealth of information by some of the best authors in the business.

Check your computer store or write:

Nibble
Box 325
Lincoln, MA 01773
(617) 259-9710

Micro

Another good source of Apple information, this magazine is written specifically for the 6502. Remember that many assembly language programs written for the PET, ATARI, or OSI computers will also work on the Apple.

Check your computer store or write:

Micro
Box 6502
Chelmsford, MA 01824
(617) 256-5515

PROGRAMMING BOOKS

Several books can help with assembly language programming for the Apple II, as well as general computer programming.

The Apple II Monitor Peeled

William Dougherty completely covers all of the routines available in the Apple II monitor ROM. As the exercises in this book show, the Apple II monitor contains many powerful routines.

Available from the author:

William E. Dougherty
14349 San Jose St.
Los Angeles, CA 91345

The Wozpak II

Although publication delays made this book somewhat dated, many of the "hidden" features of the original Apple II (Integer BASIC, non-autostart ROM) are covered in detail here. This book was written by

Steve Wozniak and is available from:

A.P.P.L.E.
304 Main Avenue. S.
Suite #300
Renton, WA 98055
(206) 271-4514

Beneath Apple DOS

This book discusses Apple DOS, including how to access it from your assembly language programs. A very thorough treatment of the subject, the book was written by Don Worth and Pieter Lechner of Quality Software. Write to:

Quality Software
6660 Reseda Blvd.
Reseda, CA 91335
(213) 344-6599

The Art of Computer Programming, Volume 1: Fundamental Algorithms

This is the first book in a series written by Donald Knuth. Available from computer stores, college book stores, or the publisher:

Addison-Wesley
South Street
Reading, MA 01867
(617) 944-3700

Software Tools

This book contains a number of universally useful algorithms. Another classic that no serious programmer should be without, this book was written by Brian W. Kernighan and P. J. Plauger. Available from most computer literature sources or from the publisher:

Addison-Wesley
South Street
Reading, MA 01867
(617) 944-3700

C
Some Apple II Assemblers

At least six assemblers are commonly available for the Apple II, including the following.

LISA ASSEMBLER

This assembler is both easy to use and powerful. It contains an extensive set of assembler directives and operates swiftly. The text insertion mode takes a little getting used to, but is convenient once mastered. This is the only assembler that uses an integrated text editor, allowing it to scan lines as they are input and print appropriate syntax error messages. For this reason, it is highly recommended for beginners. It is available from

On-Line Systems
36575 Mudge Ranch Road
Coarsegold, CA 93614
(209) 683-6858

S-C ASSEMBLER

Of all assemblers available for the Apple II, the S-C assembler behaves the most like BASIC/DOS, allowing more time to be spent learning assembly language programming, instead of how to use the assembler. Therefore, it is highly recommended for beginners. It contains a good set of assembler directives and has the ability to assemble object code directly to disk (a useful feature for long programs). The documentation, which is in two parts, is good. Order from

S-C Software
Box 280300
Dallas, TX 75228
(214) 324-2050

TLA ("The Last Assembler")

This assembler, which comes with the Apple II Language System, is one of the most powerful assemblers available for the Apple II. It uses the excellent Pascal text editor. It also supports both macro and conditional assembly — two key features for advanced assembly language programming. Unfortunately, it is only usable from within the language system. This means it cannot be used to write code for BASIC programs. It contains excellent documentation.

The TLA assembler is part of the Apple II Language System which is available from your computer store.

APPLE 6502 ASSEMBLER/EDITOR

Part of the Applesoft Tool Kit, this assembler is a disk of utilities put out by Apple. The assembler features a reasonable (but not extensive) set of assembler directives, and can generate relocatable code (a most powerful feature). The Applesoft Tool Kit with Apple 6502 Assembler/ Editor is available from your computer store.

D
LISA, Applesoft Tool Kit, And S-C Assembler Directives

In the later chapters of this book, all program listings are given in the format of the LISA assembler only. To help those using the S-C assembler or Applesoft Tool Kit, the following assembler directive comparison chart has been compiled.

LISA	S-C	Applesoft Tool Kit
ASC	.AS	ASC
ADR	.DA	DW
END	.EN	Not Used
EQU	.EQ	EQU
EPZ	.EQ	EQU
HEX	.HS	DFB
ICL	.IN	CHN
LST	.LIST ON	LST ON
NLS	.LIST OFF	LIST OFF
ORG	.OR	ORG
PAG	.PG	PAGE

E
Interfacing with the Monitor, DOS, And Applesoft BASIC

Good programming techniques dictate using available routines whenever possible. Fortunately, the Apple II has several useful routines built into it. The monitor ROM is full of usable subroutines, and DOS performs several useful functions. Applesoft contains many powerful routines.

THE MONITOR

The Apple II monitor ROM has many useful subroutines available. There are routines to input material, routines for LORES graphics, and routines to move and verify blocks of memory, beep the speaker, set up a delay, handle interrupts, and much more. Some of these routines are listed and described in the new Apple II reference manual.

Using monitor subroutines from assembly language programs is usually easy. To set up the routine, place the appropriate values in certain memory locations and registers, then use a JSR instruction to jump to the routine's entry point.

For example, there's a subroutine located at $F800 named "PLOT." It will plot one LORES "box" at the specified horizontal and vertical coordinates. To use it, first set the accumulator to the line desired (0 to 23), and the Y register to the column desired (0 to 39). Then, a JSR to PLOT will plot the point. For setting up other routines, see the references cited in Appendix B.

DOS

To access DOS from assembly language routines, some documentation on how DOS works is needed. Some information appears in the Apple DOS reference manual and other references described in Appendix B.

BASIC

Applesoft BASIC contains many powerful routines that can be called from assembly language programs. Of particular interest are the high-resolution graphics routines. A good article that explains their locations is "Applesoft II Firmware Card Hi-Res Routines," by Steve Alex, in the October 1979 issue of *Call A.P.P.L.E.*

Other types of routines available are floating point math and text interpretation routines. These are both reasonably complex topics and probably should not be attempted by beginners. However, an excellent article documenting most of Applesoft's internals is "Applesoft Internal Entry Points," by John Crossley, in the March/April 1980 issue of the *Apple Orchard.*

Of course, most BASIC/Assembly interfacing will be done the other way around (that is, calling assembly language routines from BASIC). The calling aspect is relatively straightforward; it is the passing of values that causes the trouble. An article on this topic is "Passing Values in Applesoft BASIC," by R. M. Mottola, in *Nibble*, Volume 1 No. 5.

The value of these books and magazines is obvious. They cover many of the topics you'll want to know about as you become more proficient in assembly language programming.

F
Summary of 6502 Instruction Set

Included in this appendix is a tabular representation of the 6502 instruction set. The following abbreviations are used for status headings:

S	Sign or Negative status
V	Overflow status
B	Break status
D	Decimal Mode status
I	Interrupt Disable status
Z	Zero status
C	Carry status

The following symbols are used throughout the status column:

(blank)	Operation does not affect status
X	Operation affects status
0	Operation clears status
1	Operation sets status
6	Operation reflects bit 6 of memory location

125

7	Operation reflects bit 7 of memory location
addr	Eight bits of absolute or base address
[addr+1,addr]	The address constructed from the contents of memory locations addr and addr+1. This address is used in post-indexed indirect adddressing.
addr16	Sixteen bits of absolute or base address
data	Eight bits of immediate data
disp	An 8-bit, signed address displacement
label	16-bit absolute address, destination of Jump or Jump-to-Subroutine
PC(HI)	The high-order eight bits of the Program Counter
PC(LO)	The low-order eight bits of the Program Counter
pp	The second byte of a two- or three-byte instruction object code
qq	The third byte of a three-byte object code
[ ]	Contents of the memory location designated inside the brackets. For example, [FFFE] represents the contents of memory location $FFFE_{16}$; [addr16+X] represents the contents of the location adddressed by adding the contents of register X to addr16; [SP] represents the value at the top of the Stack (contents of the memory location addressed by the Stack Pointer).
[[ ]]	Indirect addressing: the contents of the memory byte addressed by the contents of the memory location designated within the inner brackets. For example, [[addr+X]] represents the contents of a memory location addressed via pre-indexed indirect addressing.
+	Addition — either unsigned binary addition or BCD addition, depending on the condition of the Decimal Mode status.
-	Binary or BCD subtraction, performed by adding the two's complement of the subtrahend to the minuend.
—	The one's complement of the quality denoted beneath the bar; for example, $\overline{A}$ represents the complement of the contents of the accumulator; $\overline{C}$ represents the complement of the value of the Carry status.
∧	Logical AND
∨	Logical OR
⊻	Logical Exclusive-OR
←	Data is transferred in the direction of the arrow.

Table F-1. Summary of the 6502 Instruction Set

Type	Instruction	Object Code	Bytes	Clock Periods	S	V	D	I	N	C	Operation Performed
I/O and Primary Memory Reference	**LDA**										Load Accumulator from memory.
	addr	A5 pp	2	3	×				×		A←[addr] — Zero page direct
	addr,X	B5 pp	2	4	×				×		A←[addr+X] — Zero page indexed
	(addr,X)	A1 pp	2	6	×				×		A←[[addr+X]] — Pre-indexed indirect
	(addr),Y	B1 pp	2	5*	×				×		A←[[addr+1,addr]+Y] — Post-indexed indirect
	addr16	AD ppqq	3	4	×				×		A←[addr16] — Extended direct
	addr16,X or Y	11011x01 ppqq	3	4*	×				×		A←[addr16+X] or A←[addr16+Y] — Absolute indexed
	STA										Store Accumulator to memory.
	addr	85 pp	2	3							[addr]←A — Zero page direct
	addr,X	95 pp	2	4							[addr+X]←A — Zero page indexed
	(addr,X)	81 pp	2	6							[[addr+X]]←A — Pre-indexed indirect
	(addr),Y	91 pp	2	6							[[addr+1,addr]+Y]←A — Post-indexed indirect
	addr16	8D ppqq	3	4							[addr16]←A — Extended direct
	addr16,X or Y	10011x01 ppqq	3	5							[addr16+X]←A or [addr16+Y]←A — Absolute indexed
	LDX										Load Index Register X from memory. Index through Register Y only.
	addr	A6 pp	2	3	×				×		X←[addr] — Zero page direct
	addr,Y	B6 pp	2	4	×				×		X←[addr+Y] — Zero page indexed
	addr16	AE ppqq	3	4	×				×		X←[addr16] — Extended direct
	addr16,Y	BE ppqq	3	4*	×				×		X←[addr16+Y] — Absolute indexed
	STX										Store Index Register X to memory. Index through Register Y only.
	addr	86 pp	2	3							[addr]←X — Zero page direct
	addr,Y	96 pp	2	4							[addr+Y]←X — Zero page indexed
	addr16	8E ppqq	3	4							[addr16]←X — Extended direct
	LDY										Load Index Register Y from memory. Index through Register X only.
	addr	A4 pp	2	3	×				×		Y←[addr] — Zero page direct
	addr,X	B4 pp	2	4	×				×		Y←[addr+X] — Zero page indexed
	addr16	AC ppqq	3	4	×				×		Y←[addr16] — Extended direct
	addr16,X	BC ppqq	3	4*	×				×		Y←[addr16+X] — Absolute indexed

Status columns: S V D I N C

* Add one clock period if page boundary is crossed. In the object code, "x" designates the index register: x = 0 for Register Y, x = 1 for Register X.

Table F-1. Summary of the 6502 Instruction Set (Continued)

Type	Instruction	Object Code	Bytes	Clock Periods	S	V	D	I	Z	C	Operation Performed
I/O and Primary Memory Reference (Continued)	**STY**										Store Index Register Y to memory. Index through Register X only.
	addr	84 pp	2	3							$[addr] \leftarrow Y$ Zero page direct
	addr,X	94 pp	2	4							$[addr+X] \leftarrow Y$ Zero page indexed
	addr16	8C ppqq	3	4							$[addr16] \leftarrow Y$ Extended direct
Secondary Memory Reference (Memory Operate)	**ADC**										Add contents of memory location, with carry, to those of Accumulator.
	addr	65 pp	2	3	×	×			×	×	$A \leftarrow A+[addr]+C$ Zero page direct
	addr,X	75 pp	2	4	×	×			×	×	$A \leftarrow A+[addr+X]+C$ Zero page indexed
	(addr,X)	61 pp	2	6	×	×			×	×	$A \leftarrow A+[[addr+X]]+C$ Pre-indexed indirect
	(addr),Y	71 pp	2	5*	×	×			×	×	$A \leftarrow A+[[addr+1, addr]+Y]+C$ Post-indexed indirect
	addr16	6D ppqq	3	4	×	×			×	×	$A \leftarrow A+[addr16]+C$ Extended direct
	addr16,X or Y	01111x01 ppqq	3	4*	×	×			×	×	$A \leftarrow A+[addr16+X]+C$ or $A \leftarrow A+[addr16+Y]+C$ Absolute indexed
											[Zero flag is not valid in Decimal Mode].
	AND										AND contents of Accumulator with those of memory location.
	addr	25 pp	2	3	×				×		$A \leftarrow A \wedge [addr]$ Zero page direct
	addr,X	35 pp	2	4	×				×		$A \leftarrow A \wedge [addr+X]$ Zero page indexed
	(addr,X)	21 pp	2	6	×				×		$A \leftarrow A \wedge [[addr+X]]$ Pre-indexed indirect
	(addr),Y	31 pp	2	5*	×				×		$A \leftarrow A \wedge [[addr+1, addr]+Y]$ Post-indexed indirect
	addr16	2D ppqq	3	4	×				×		$A \leftarrow A \wedge [addr16]$ Extended direct
	addr16,X or Y	00111x01 ppqq	3	4*	×				×		$A \leftarrow A \wedge [addr16+X]$ or $A \leftarrow A \wedge [addr16+Y]$ Absolute indexed
	BIT										AND contents of Accumulator with those of memory location. Only the status bits are affected.
	addr	24 pp	2	3	7	6			×		$A \wedge [addr]$ Zero page direct
	addr16	2C ppqq	3	4	7	6			×		$A \wedge [addr16]$ Extended direct

* Add one clock period if page boundary is crossed. In the object code, "x" designates the Index register: x = 0 for Register Y, x = 1 for Register X.

Table F-1. Summary of the 6502 Instruction Set (Continued)

Type	Instruction	Object Code	Bytes	Clock Periods	S	V	D	I	Z	C	Operation Performed
Secondary Memory Reference (Memory Operate) (Continued)	CMP										Compare contents of Accumulator with those of memory location. Only the status bits are affected.
	addr	C5 pp	2	3	x				x	x	A−[addr] — Zero page direct
	addr,X	D5 pp	2	4	x				x	x	A−[addr+X] — Zero page indexed
	(addr,X)	C1 pp	2	6	x				x	x	A−[[addr+X]] — Pre-indexed indirect
	(addr),Y	D1 pp	2	5*	x				x	x	A−[[addr]+1, addr]+Y] — Post-indexed indirect
	addr16	CD ppqq	3	4	x				x	x	A−[addr16] — Extended direct
	addr16,X or Y	11011x01 ppqq	3	4*	x				x	x	A−[addr16+X] or A−[addr16+Y] — Absolute indexed
	EOR										Exclusive-OR contents of Accumulator with those of memory location.
	addr	45 pp	2	3	x				x		A—A⊻[addr] — Zero page direct
	addr,X	55 pp	2	4	x				x		A—A⊻[addr+X] — Zero page indexed
	(addr,X)	41 pp	2	6	x				x		A—A⊻[[addr+X]] — Pre-indexed indirect
	(addr),Y	51 pp	2	5*	x				x		A—A⊻[[addr+1, addr]+Y] — Post-indexed indirect
	addr16	4D ppqq	3	4	x				x		A—A⊻[addr16] — Extended direct
	addr16,X or Y	01011x01 ppqq	3	4*	x				x		A—A⊻[addr16+X] or A—A⊻[addr16+Y] — Absolute indexed
	ORA										OR contents of Accumulator with those of memory location.
	addr	05 pp	2	3	x				x		A—A∨[addr] — Zero page direct
	addr,X	15 pp	2	4	x				x		A—A∨[addr+X] — Zero page indexed
	(addr,X)	01 pp	2	6	x				x		A—A∨[[addr+X]] — Pre-indexed indirect
	(addr),Y	11 pp	2	5*	x				x		A—A∨[[addr+1, addr]+Y] — Post-indexed indirect
	addr16	0D ppqq	3	4	x				x		A—A∨[addr16] — Extended direct
	addr16,X or Y	00011x01 ppqq	3	4*	x				x		A—A∨[addr16+X] or A—A∨[addr16+Y] — Absolute indexed

* Add one clock period if page boundary is crossed. In the object code, "x" designates the Index register: x = 0 for Register Y, x = 1 for Register X.

Table F-1. Summary of the 6502 Instruction Set (Continued)

Type	Instruction	Object Code	Bytes	Clock Periods	S	V	D	I	Z	C	Operation Performed
Secondary Memory Reference (Memory Operate) (Continued)	**SBC**										Subtract contents of memory location, with borrow, from contents of Accumultor.
	addr	E5 pp	2	3	x	x			x	x	$A \leftarrow A - [addr] - \bar{C}$ — Zero page direct
	addr,X	F5 pp	2	4	x	x			x	x	$A \leftarrow A - [addr+X] - \bar{C}$ — Zero page indexed
	(addr,X)	E1 pp	2	6	x	x			x	x	$A \leftarrow A - [[addr+X]] - \bar{C}$ — Pre-indexed indirect
	(addr),Y	F1 pp	2	5*	x	x			x	x	$A \leftarrow A - [[addr+1,addr]+Y] - \bar{C}$ — Post-indexed indirect
	addr16	ED ppqq	3	4	x	x			x	x	$A \leftarrow A - [addr16] - \bar{C}$ — Extended direct
	addr16,X or Y	11111x01 ppqq	3	4*	x	x			x	x	$A \leftarrow A - [addr16+Y] - \bar{C}$ or $A \leftarrow A - [addr16+X] - \bar{C}$ — Absolute indexed (Note that Carry value is the complement of the borrow.)
	INC										Increment contents of memory location. Index through Register X only.
	addr	E6 pp	2	5	x				x		$[addr] \leftarrow [addr]+1$ — Zero page direct
	addr,X	F6 pp	2	6	x				x		$[addr+X] \leftarrow [addr+X]+1$ — Zero page indexed
	addr16	EE ppqq	3	6	x				x		$[addr16] \leftarrow [addr16]+1$ — Extended direct
	addr16,X	FE ppqq	3	7	x				x		$[addr16+X] \leftarrow [addr16+X]+1$ — Absolute indexed
	DEC										Decrement contents of memory location. Index through Register X only.
	addr	C6 pp	2	5	x				x		$[addr] \leftarrow [addr]-1$ — Zero page direct
	addr,X	D6 pp	2	6	x				x		$[addr+X] \leftarrow [addr+X]-1$ — Zero page indexed
	addr16	CE ppqq	3	6	x				x		$[addr16] \leftarrow [addr16]-1$ — Extended direct
	addr16,X	DE ppqq	3	7	x				x		$[addr16+X] \leftarrow [addr16+X]-1$ — Absolute indexed
	CPX										Compare contents of X register with those of memory location. Only the status flags are affected.
	addr	E4 pp	2	3	x				x	x	$X-[addr]$ — Zero page direct
	addr16	EC ppqq	3	4	x				x	x	$X-[addr16]$ — Extended direct
	CPY										Compare contents of Y register with those of memory location. Only the status flags are affected.
	addr	C4 pp	2	3	x				x	x	$Y-[addr]$ — Zero page direct
	addr16	CC ppqq	3	4	x				x	x	$Y-[addr16]$ — Extended direct

* Add one clock period if page boundary is crossed. In the object code, "x" designates the Index register: x = 0 for Register Y, x = 1 for Register X.

Table F-1. Summary of the 6502 Instruction Set (Continued)

Type	Instruction	Object Code	Bytes	Clock Periods	S	V	D	I	Z	C	Operation Performed
Secondary Memory Reference (Memory Operate) (Continued)	ROL										Rotate contents of memory location one bit left through Carry. Index through Register X only.
	addr	26 pp	2	5	x				x	x	[addr]
	addr.X	36 pp	2	6	x				x	x	[addr+X]
	addr16	2E ppqq	3	6	x				x	x	[addr16]
	addr16.X	3E ppqq	3	7	x				x	x	[addr16+X]
	ROR										Rotate contents of memory location one bit right, through Carry. Index through Register X only.
	addr	66 pp	2	5	x				x	x	[addr]
	addr.X	76 pp	2	6	x				x	x	[addr+X]
	addr16	6E pp	3	6	x				x	x	[addr16]
	addr16.X	7E ppqq	3	7	x				x	x	[addr16+X]
	ASL										Arithmetic shift left contents of memory location. Index through Register X only.
	addr	06 pp	2	5	x				x	x	[addr]
	addr.X	16 pp	2	6	x				x	x	[addr+X]
	addr16	0E ppqq	3	6	x				x	x	[addr16]
	addr16.X	1E ppqq	3	7	x				x	x	[addr16+X]

Table F-1. Summary of the 6502 Instruction Set (Continued)

Type	Instruction	Object Code	Bytes	Clock Periods	S	V	D	I	Z	C	Operation Performed
Secondary Memory Ref. (Memory Operate) (Cont.)	**LSR**										Logical shift right contents of memory location. Index through Register X only. [addr] [addr+X] [addr16] [addr16,X]
	addr	46 pp	2	5	0				X	X	
	addr,X	56 pp	2	6	0				X	X	
	addr16	4E ppqq	3	6	0				X	X	
	addr16,X	5E ppqq	3	7	0				X	X	
Immediate	LDA data	A9 pp	2	2	X				X		Load Accumulator with immediate data. A—data
	LDX data	A2 pp	2	2	X				X		Load Index Register X with immediate data. X—data
	LDY data	A0 pp	2	2	X				X		Load Index Register Y with immediate data. Y—data

Table F-1. Summary of the 6502 Instruction Set (Continued)

Type	Instruction	Object Code	Bytes	Clock Periods	S	V	D	I	Z	C	Operation Performed
Immediate Operate	ADC data	69 pp	2	2	X	X			X	X	Add immediate with Carry, to Accumulator. The Zero flag is not valid in Decimal Mode. A→A+data+C
	AND data	29 pp	2	2	X				X		AND immediate with Accumulator. A→A∧data
	CMP data	C9 pp	2	2	X				X	X	Compare immediate with Accumulator. Only the status flags are affected. A-data
	EOR data	49 pp	2	2	X				X		Exclusive-OR immediate with Accumulator. A→A⊻data
	ORA data	09 pp	2	2	X				X		OR immediate with Accumulator. A→A∨data
	SBC data	E9 pp	2	2	X	X			X	X	Subtract immediate, with borrow, from Accumulator. A→A-data-C̄ (Note that Carry value is the complement of the borrow.)
	CPX data	E0 pp	2	2	X				X	X	Compare immediate with Index Register X. Only the status flags are affected. X-data
	CPY data	C0 pp	2	2	X				X	X	Compare immediate with Index Register Y. Only the status flags are affected. Y-data
Jump	JMP label	4C ppqq	3	3							Jump to new location, using extended or indirect addressing. PC→label or PC→[label]
	(label)	6C ppqq	3	5							

Table F-1. Summary of the 6502 Instruction Set (Continued)

Type	Instruction	Object Code	Bytes	Clock Periods	Status S	V	D	I	Z	C	Operation Performed
Branch on Condition											Note the following for all Branch-on-Condition instructions:
											If the condition is satisfied, the displacement is added to the Program Counter after the Program Counter has been incremented to point to the instruction following the Branch instruction.
	BCC disp	90 pp	2	2**							Branch relative if Carry flag is cleared.
											If C=0, then PC←PC+disp
	BCS disp	B0 pp	2	2**							Branch relative if Carry flag is set.
											If C=1, then PC←PC+disp
	BEQ disp	F0 pp	2	2**							Branch relative if result is equal to zero.
											If Z=1, then PC←PC+disp
	BMI disp	30 pp	2	2**							Branch relative if result is negative.
											If S=1, then PC←PC+disp
	BNE disp	D0 pp	2	2**							Branch relative if result is not zero.
											If Z=0, then PC←PC+disp
	BPL disp	10 pp	2	2**							Branch relative if result is positive.
											If S=0, then PC←PC+disp
	BVC disp	50 pp	2	2**							Branch relative if Overflow flag is cleared.
											If V = 0, then PC←PC+disp
	BVS disp	70 pp	2	2**							Branch relative if Overflow flag is set.
											If V=1, then PC←PC+disp

**Add one clock period if branch occurs to location in same page; add two clock periods if branch to another page occurs.

Table F-1. Summary of the 6502 Instruction Set (Continued)

Type	Instruction	Object Code	Bytes	Clock Periods	S	V	D	I	Z	C	Operation Performed
Subroutine Call and Return	JSR label	20 ppqq	3	6							Jump to subroutine beginning at address given in bytes 2 and 3 of the instruction. Note that the stored Program Counter points to the last byte of the JSR instruction. [SP]→PC(HI) [SP−1]→PC(LO) SP→SP−2 PC→label
	RTS	60	1	6							Return from subroutine, incrementing Program Counter to point to the instruction after the JSR which called the routine. PC(LO)→[SP+1] PC(HI)→[SP+2] SP→SP+2 PC→PC+1
Register-Register Move	TAX	AA	1	2	X				X		Move Accumulator contents to Index Register X. X→A
	TXA	8A	1	2	X				X		Move contents of Index Register X to Accumulator. A→X
	TAY	A8	1	2	X				X		Move Accumulator contents to Index Register Y. Y→A
	TYA	98	1	2	X				X		Move contents of Index Register Y to Accumulator, A→Y
	TSX	BA	1	2	X				X		Move contents of Stack Pointer to Index Register X. X→SP
	TXS	9A	1	2							Move contents of Index Register X to Stack Pointer. SP→X

Table F-1. Summary of the 6502 Instruction Set (Continued)

Type	Instruction	Object Code	Bytes	Clock Periods	S	V	D	I	Z	C	Operation Performed
Register Operate	DEX	CA	1	2	X				X		Decrement contents of Index Register X. X←X−1
	DEY	88	1	2	X				X		Decrement contents of Index Register Y. Y←Y−1
	INX	E8	1	2	X				X		Increment contents of Index Register X. X←X+1
	INY	C8	1	2	X				X		Increment contents of Index Register Y. Y←Y+1
	ROL A	2A	1	2	X				X	X	Rotate contents of Accumulator left through Carry.
	ROR A	6A	1	2	X					X	Rotate contents of Accumulator right, through Carry.
	ASL A	0A	1	2	X				X	X	Arithmetic shift left contents of Accumulator.
	LSR A	4A	1	2	0				X	X	Logical shift right contents of Accumulator.

Table F-1. Summary of the 6502 Instruction Set (Continued)

Type	Instruction	Object Code	Bytes	Clock Periods	S	V	D	I	Z	C	Operation Performed
Stack	PHA	48	1	3							Push Accumulator contents onto Stack. [SP]←A SP←SP−1
	PLA	68	1	4	×				×		Load Accumulator from top of Stack ("Pull"). A←[SP+1] SP←SP+1
	PHP	08	1	3							Push Status register contents onto Stack. [SP]←P SP←SP−1
	PLP	28	1	4	×	×	×	×	×	×	Load Status register from top of Stack ("Pull"). P←[SP+1] SP←SP+1
Interrupt	CLI	58	1	2				0			Enable interrupts by clearing interrupt disable bit of Status register. I←0
	SEI	78	1	2				1			Disable interrupts I←1
	RTI	40	1	6	×	×	×	×	×	×	Return from interrupt; restore Status P←[SP+1] PC(LO)←[SP+2] PC(HI)←[SP+3] SP←SP+3 PC←PC+1
	BRK	00	1	7				1			Programmed interrupt. BRK cannot be disabled. The Program Counter is incremented twice before it is saved on the Stack. [SP]←PC(HI) [SP−1]←PC(LO) [SP−2]←P SP←SP−3 PC(HI)←[FFFF] PC(LO)←[FFFE] I←1 B←1

Table F-1. Summary of the 6502 Instruction Set (Continued)

Type	Instruction	Object Code	Bytes	Clock Periods	Status S	Status V	Status D	Status I	Status Z	Status C	Operation Performed
Status	CLC	18	1	2						0	Clear Carry flag C—0
	SEC	38	1	2						1	Set Carry flag C—1
	CLD	D8	1	2			0				Clear Decimal Mode D—0
	SED	F8	1	2			1				Set Decimal Mode D—1
	CLV	B8	1	2		0					Clear Overflow flag V—0
	NOP	EA	1	2							No Operation

Index

139

Other OSBORNE/McGraw-Hill Publications